HAPPY CLIMBING TELLS NO TALES

AND OTHER MOUNTAIN STORIES TALL AND SHORT

HAPPY CLIMBING TELLS NO TALES

AND OTHER MOUNTAIN STORIES TALL AND SHORT

Judith Brown

OPEN MOUNTAIN

Open Mountain
1 The Pumphouse
Gt Broughton
Cockermouth

Cumbria CA13 0YX

ISBN: 978-0955498-008

Typeset in 12pt Bembo by Troubador Publishing Ltd, Leicester, UK
Cover design by Sarah Spalding

OPEN MOUNTAIN

*These stories are dedicated to the many companions
with whom I have shared adventures in the
mountains and to the members of the Women
Mountains Words and other friends whose critical
encouragement gave me the courage to share them.*

CONTENTS

FANCY BOOTS NEVER WORE NO HELMET

Hunched at the end of the bench, he absorbed his partner's news in silence. He spat tobacco into the fire and pinched the ends of a cigarette together with his fingers. Not looking at the other man but concentrating only upon his smoke, Tincan lit the roll-up, drawing on it as he tossed the match into the fire and slipped the makings back into his jacket pocket.

"Tomorrow you reckon?"

"Sure – tomorrow."

Tincan put his feet up on the table. It was ancient and someone had forced a penny into one of its cracks. He assumed a proprietorial air.

"Just them two?"

"Just them. That's what I heard. Just Fancy Boots and Joe Beswick. He's hard enough "

Tincan turned his head and looked at the other man as if he was dim-witted.

"Shit, Billy, you'd be hard too, hanging around with Fancy Boots."

Billy grinned. "Yeah, I reckon."

Tincan flicked the ash from the cigarette onto the rug under the table, making his small addition to its patina of ground-in food, mud and spilt beer.

"So you know what this means?"

"Early start is what it means to me."

He lifted his feet from the table and unfolded himself from the bench. He threw the chewed end of the cigarette into the fire.

"Best get some shut-eye then. Up by sparrow-fart tomorrow and ready to go."

The dawn was a pale streak of light against the sky just visible beyond the last of the hills as they rolled down into the moorland, sliding away towards the plain and the sea. To the west all was black, the mountains giant panthers hunched and slumbered, ready to pounce as they were touched by the sun and prodded by disrespectful humans. Billy had the engine running in the old pick-up and Tincan threw his gear onto the flatbed and hauled himself into the passenger seat.

"This old girl don't get no better. Sounds like she smokes more'n I do."

Billy let off the hand-brake and the van chugged off down the rocky track, wheezing mightily, like she resented being roused from her dreams of monster truck racing.

"She goes" said Billy "Don't reckon you can ask more'n that of a machine."

They drove in silence, there being no discussion to be usefully had about what they were about to do. There had been plenty of talk in the weeks working up to this. Talk that made the thing easy, words that wound round difficulties like ivy to a tree, finding holds where there were none, stamping the certainty of success in black type in some future guidebook where in reality there was at best informed guesswork and at worst ignorance. Later would come time for more words, the record of the thing done, making a reality of what otherwise only they would know, understated words of the write-up, and the tales of pub gossip. But for the moment, words were not enough. Now the only thing was to do it and to do it before anyone else did.

They stopped at a pull-in by the track. Billy parked at an angle.

"They won't get in here. They'll have to walk the half mile up the road."

"They'll know it's us. Fancy Boots might just put a stray rock through the windshield." Tincan shouldered his pack. "It's what I'd do."

Billy locked the cab and put the keys into the top-pocket of his sack before lifting it up onto his back.

"But you're a goddamned son-of-a-bitch."

"I guess so."

They let themselves through the gate and started the trudge up the hill neither man noticing the spread of the morning light as it lit the grass. And neither noticing either the stream tumbling from the darkness above down into the bright day. Both were wrapped in the concentration of one foot in front of the other, keeping a tight pace, making time up the hill, trying to think only of the getting there and not of what had to be done.

They covered ground quickly, skilled at picking the best line, leaving the worn trail to cut across contourlines straight to the crag. Tincan stopped briefly, scanning the hillside beneath them.

"Ain't no-one behind us."

"Well, they know it's ours by rights, mebbe they've decided to back off."

Tincan spat onto the grass. "Yeah. Mebbe." They pressed on.

3

About an hour had passed by the time the cliff came into view. Still in shadow it was dark and steep and had the air of a being withdrawn. It was a feeling the men knew well.

"It'll go."

"It'll go."

As they got nearer, the sun was creeping onto the base of the crag. Tincan stopped dead in his tracks.

"Shit!"

Billy stopped, following his partner's gaze.

"Tell me I ain't seeing what I'm seeing."

Not far from the bottom of the crag, but definitely making progress up it, a white helmet showed against the rock.

"Bastards! Must've bivvied."

"They ain't but a few feet up it."

Tincan looked at Billy as though he might hit him.

"You want I should go get my gun and shoot 'em off?"

Billy shrugged. "There must be some way of stopping them."

"What we do is go like hot shit off a shovel and stop her starting off. Joe's good but he ain't crazy."

"You reckon that's Joe in front?"

"Must be. Fancy Boots never wore no helmet." Tincan grinned. "Rather a cracked head than mussed up hair."

They ran up the hillside, hearts pumping and breathe rasping, covering the remaining distance in minutes. The woman watched them come. She paid out the twin ropes and casually turned her head towards the climber above.

"We've got company", was all she said.

The guys threw their sacks at her feet, which were bare.

Something sparkled through the grass where she was standing.

It was her boots.

Billy bent over, panting to get his breath back, riled at the effort, and at her.

The woman smiled. "Hi, guys. Want to make the second ascent?"

"We worked this route and you know it."

"Thanks, how kind of you."

Billy looked up the crag. Joe was getting on with climbing, ignoring those below.

"F**king get yourself back down here, pal!" Billy managed to yell between laboured breaths.

Tincan said nothing. He squatted on his rucksack, rolling a cigarette, eyeing the ropes and the gear. He watched Joe place a runner and clip into it, searching for the next holds. Then he turned and smiled.

"Fancy Boots, how're you doin'?"

"Doin' fine, Tincan. You?"

He drew on the roll-up and lay back, cushioning his head on his arm.

"Fine, I guess."

"Fine if it wasn't for you two bastards stealing our route" gasped Billy.

"Hey, cool it, Billy Boy. That's no way to speak to a lady."

The woman snorted.

"Same old Tincan."

"Same old Fancy Boots."

Billy picked up his sack and tipped the gear out with an aggressive shake.

"How come *you're* so f**king relaxed all of a sudden?"

Tincan was watching the slow progress on the route above him.

"It's the female charm that soothes the raging breast" he said and went on smoking and watching.

Above, Joe had come to a standstill. He was bridged out awkwardly with his right hand creeping over the rock, trying to find something to make upward movement possible. He dusted chalk onto a pinch-grip, then wiped his palm on his trouser-leg and dipped back into the chalk-bag. The sun was on him now and the day was warming fast. They were too far below to hear his breathing but they could sense it, a stretching of ribs and muscle over pulsing lungs, tensing the air almost to snapping point. No-one spoke. The woman was fixed on the control of the ropes, ready to pay-out if Joe made the move successfully, to take-in fast if he did not. Billy looked at the climber and then he looked at Tincan who appeared to be asleep, except for the slight tension in the fingers keeping the ash from his cigarette butt from falling on his chest.

Joe pinched the fin of rock and moved up. They could not see what he was standing on. His legs started to tremble, shaking with the strain of pressing them down into almost nothing. The woman broke the silence.

"Can you get something in, Joe?"

His voice was distant. "No, nothing".

"He's at the crux" said Billy. He glanced at Tincan. "We did think this bit would be the crux, didn't we?"

Tincan ignored him.

Joe's whole body was beginning to shake. "Watch me!"

The woman stood firm, legs apart, knees bent. Her toes dug into the turf, preparing to absorb the shock of a long fall.

"I've got you. You're OK. You're not going anywhere."

"Jesus Christ! I need some gear!"

Billy looked at Tincan. "He's gonna take one helluva dive from there."

Tincan didn't move a muscle.

"I reckon you may be right" he said.

The seconds stretched out slowly as they waited for what was about to happen, counting silent heartbeats to the fall.

Joe made a wild lunge upwards and was off, flying feet-first, a long way down, flipping over, diving, and then the rope tugging him back as it came tight onto the runner. Joe stopped. He was hanging upside-down.

Below, Fancy Boots was braced against the rock a few feet above the ground, ropes locked off stiffly in the belay plate.

"You OK, Joe?!"

Joe was struggling to right himself. "I think so. I don't know. Something hurts."

Tincan roused himself and stood beneath Fancy Boots. He reached up and took hold of her naked feet in his hands. She still had the scar on her ankle, he noticed. "Just gonna bring you back down to earth, darlin'"

He held her steady as she made contact with the turf again. Fancy Boots lowered Joe to the ground. He sat on the grass and allowed Billy to untie the ropes from his harness.

He took off his helmet and examined it. There were clear scratch marks where he had scraped his head. He looked across at Fancy Boots sorting out the ropes and at Tincan who was helping her.

"You should wear one of these" Joe said.

"Too sensible for me. Anyway, where does it hurt?"

"It's my ankle, I think I twisted it, cracked it maybe."

"Do you think you can walk off OK? Shall I go call the rescue?"

"Just let me rest it a while. I think I might manage on my own. I've gone twenty bloody years without the rescue – I'd like to keep a clean licence."

Tincan had tipped up his rucksack and was gearing up, arranging wires and cams and tie-offs, the assorted paraphernalia of climbing, onto the loops of his harness and onto the bandolier that hung across his chest.

Billy looked at Joe rubbing his ankle then shot a look at Tincan.

"You still aiming to do this thing?"

"It's what we came for."

"What about helping Joe?"

Tincan regarded the man on the ground.

"You ain't bleeding to death, are you mate?"

"I'll live. You go ahead."

Tincan hitched up his harness so that it sat tight around his waist.

"I intend to." He handed the ends of his ropes to Billy. "Perhaps you'd better tie yourself onto something. If I start flying off this thing I don't want you coming up to meet me."

The woman gave him a cool look. "Somehow, I don't think you'll take a fall as big as Joe's."

He grinned at her, dipping his hands in his chalk-bag, smearing them white.

"We gonna see them boots of yours in action today?"

"Just try to stop me."

He set off up the rock moving smoothly and with confidence, removing the gear that Joe had put in, replacing it with his own. When he got to the wire that had stopped the fall he tugged it. It failed to move so he clipped the rope into it. He pulled up on the pinch grip, stretching his legs into a wide bridge. Taking a small brass wire from his harness he reached high up to his left. The wire seated neatly into a fine crack. He clipped the other rope.

Fancy Boots was sat with Joe, bathing his ankle with a water-soaked handkerchief but watching the climb over her shoulder. She addressed Billy. "He knew about that placement, didn't he?"

"Yeah, we cleaned it out. We knew that would be the hardest move so we wanted to make sure there would be something there."

The woman exchanged glances with Joe, who just shrugged.

The rest of the climb wasn't easy, but Tincan made his way up the route steadily. At the top he went a long way back to get a good belay, then re-emerged at the edge.

"Who's coming up first?"

The woman grabbed one of the ropes. "Me, on blue! Just let me get my boots on."

Billy watched as she squeezed her feet into her rockboots. They were elaborately decorated with a bead trim around the ankle and rhinestones on the tongue. He'd never seen anything like them.

"They sure are fancy"

"Did it all myself."

"How long do they last?"

"They wear out as fast as anybody's. I just take the stuff off and do the next pair the same."

Billy shook his head. "Why?"

"'Cos it makes 'em magic, that's why. Ain't never gonna fall off with these beauties on my feet"

Joe and Billy watched the boots at work, the neat way she used her feet, her precision climbing.

Tincan regarded her from above, seeing the dark hair, the way she pushed her fringe from her eyes as she studied the rock. He took the rope in and felt it connecting to her waist and hips.

9

He swallowed and looked away, out to the bright horizon where the sharp mountains flowed in their clear and separate ranges down to the sea. And the sea glittered like a vast broken mirror, reflecting nothing but the unobtainable dreams of men. The smell of gorse pollen warming in the sun filled the air. Tincan suddenly felt his eyes begin to water.

"You're going well there, Fancy Boots" he called.

"I know" she replied.

As she came to the hard moves, he felt the pull on the rope as she stretched into the bridge, her legs appearing almost horizontal as he looked down upon them. He saw the long reach with her right hand, sensed as her fingers pinched the hold, and willed her to commit to it. She did and with a grunt of effort she was through the crux. After that the elegance returned, the glittery boots working their magic on the rock.

Soon she was at the top, lying on the grass beside him. He turned to her as he brought in Billy's rope.

"So? Good route?"

"Good route."

"Happy?"

"I'd be happier if Joe hadn't of fallen off."

"You mean you'd rather have climbed it with him?"

"Don't be a pig, Tincan. Maybe we shouldn't have tried to steal the route, but all's fair in war and climbing, so they say."

"Even me not telling Joe about that placement at the crux?"

She took off her boots, running her fingers over the beads, feeling them like a message in Braille that only she could understand.

"There's no way we could have known about it. Anyway we wanted to do it completely clean. We went prepared to make our own way and that's what we did."

Tincan let out a thin laugh.

"Ha! Completely clean as in me and Billy had already cleaned it for you, you mean."

He took the rope in tightly as he felt Billy teetering up the crux moves.

"Well, yeah,O.K. But Joe could have hurt himself ......"

Tincan coughed and spat. "He ain't dead."

The woman stood up. "Neither are we, Tincan, but we're both a bit battered round the edges."

"That's what comes of trusting to fancy boots and not wearing a helmet."

He was taking the rope in quickly now. Billy would be joining them soon.

"So, the thing is, once we've got Joe to hospital or home or wherever, are you going to join me for a drink?"

She dropped down onto her haunches behind him, placing a hand on either shoulder. "Brian Jones, I think you are one ruthless, selfish son-of-a-bitch who doesn't give a damn about anyone else."

He tilted his face up to hers. "This I know, but it is not an answer to my question, Julie Thomas."

She stood back up and placed her hands on his head. "I'll take a drink with you."

He grinned, freed one hand from the ropes, and grabbed her ankle and squeezed it, running his thumb along the faint white scar.

"That still bother you?"

"I suppose it might when the pins wear out."

"You really scared me that day, you know."

She drummed her fingers on his head.

"Sorry if I upset you. You managed to hide it well, I'd say."

At that instant, Billy pulled over the top. He looked at Tincan's hand as it released from the woman's ankle.

"She twisted hers too?"

Tincan laughed. "Remember what I said this morning? Fancy Boots never wore no helmet?"

"I ain't got a brain worth a damn to put in it."

"That's OK, darlin'. Ain't your brains I'm after."

She ignored him and heard Billy saying how the climb wasn't that hard really and Tincan not replying but coming to stand next to her as they coiled the ropes. She watched as he made his roll-up and felt the brief touch of his fingers on her back as they started off down the hillside. The slope was broad and rolling and Tincan walked beside her, his hand on the boots that swung from her harness.

TROLL CLIMB

Grey rock frozen in its giant wave-break against the pale sky. Grey rock in an endless sweep like a castle wall in a horror movie. Grey rock that scuffed his finger ends, biting its small sharp teeth of flint into his skin, its grimness draining the colour from his flesh, seeping dull red into the cliff like dried blood, knuckles white with strain.

He breathed, a deep snatch of breathe like it was his first breathe, as if preparing for this relentless tsunami rock to break upon his head and drag him under. It was cold, bone-cold, deep-cold, ancient cold, the cliff raising its face to the north and clouds heavy with snow, the sun a fleeting presence of the northland summer evening, giving light but little warmth.

He tamped in a small rock on wire, tugging it tight into a crack, fumbling with numb fingers to feed the rope into the gate of the karabiner. Metal clicked on metal as it snapped shut. He tried to relax and took one hand at a time off the rock to breath upon his finger ends. They were ragged with the rock and waxy with the cold, slow in everything except the chill fire of pain.

He climbed on, deliberating moves, stiff and heavy, his body bulky with the layers of clothing that trapped in what little warmth there was. He glanced down to where the twin ropes fell vertically below him, dropping from his sight into the mist, down to his partner invisible far below, holding his life in her hands. They dragged heavily at his waist. Impatiently the climber snatched at them, loosening the clutch of their weight

13

upon him. He shouted, How much rope? His words dropped into the silence.

He found a big hold, a flake of rock prized from the wall by the centuries' working of ice and thaw. He pulled it and thumped it and shook it. It seemed solid. He struggled to lift a sling over his head and arm, catching it against the rucksack, cursing it softly, the swear words almost manifesting in the smoke of his breath as it hit the cold air. Carefully he placed the sling over the flake and clipped himself to it. He fanned the gear that hung across his chest from the bandolier and selected a camming device. Drawing back its bars he inserted its narrow profile into the crack behind the flake and watched as its cams opened within the fissure and bit into its sides. Fumbling a knot into the yellow rope he clipped it into the device. He looked for something else, some third placement where another piece of gear could share the strain of any fall. He did not find it. At last he settled himself on small footholds and pulled his gloves from the breast of his jacket. His fingers were so stiff he needed the help of his teeth to pull them on.

OK! I'm safe!

Again the words were swallowed by the mist. He had no hope that she had heard them. He tugged hard three times, the pre-arranged signal that he was safely belayed and started to take in the remaining rope. It was hard work at first, the ropes solid and heavy. It had been a long pitch. There could have been little rope left at his partner's feet. He expected them to come taut very quickly as he connected with her harness. He kept on hauling. He wondered whether she was already climbing, not waiting for the tugs that would signal that he had her safe and that she could begin her ascent. As quickly as he could with gloved hands, he fed the ropes through the belay plate and then started again the task of taking in the rope. It began to pull up easily. The woman was a good climber but this was steep rock and cold enough to freeze the body into slowness, especially one that had been waiting on the ledge below for at least an hour. It was not possible that she could climb this fast, faster than he could take the rope in, and yet in it came, great loops of it, spilling over his boots and hanging back down the cliff, puddles of brilliant colour in the dim light.

The half-points of the ropes pulled through the plate, the sudden thickening made by the tape markers jamming momentarily, then on the rope sped through his hands, faster than his tired arms could haul it.

You'll have to slow down! he yelled, but on came the ropes, an abstract movement of colour in the frozen silence, rising too soon through the karabiner of the runner below, pulling right through the karabiner below, the red and yellow tails flicking through and free. He froze in mid-haul and looked down at the empty ends of the ropes hanging beneath him.

Sophie!

It started to snow, watery flakes that settled on his lashes and made his eyes water. There was no sound not even of the wind. Snow and cloud settled around him. He called again into the silence. Reluctantly, fearful of what he might find, he pulled the final few metres of rope up to him. He held their ends in his hand and looked at them. They were complete and undamaged, with the white end tapes wrapped firmly around them. They had not been chopped through by falling rock, nor abraded by being pulled over its roughness, nor had they been cut through with a knife. They had been untied. For some reason Sophie had undone the ropes from her harness and was still on the ledge below. He shouted until his voice cracked and he could shout no more. It was as if he was alone on the mountain with nothing but grey rock and two empty ropes for company.

He considered his options and found only one. He would have to trust in the solidity of the flake and of the gear cammed behind it and abseil back down the way he had come, back down to the ledge to find Sophie, to find out what the hell was going on.

His anger rose quickly to warm him as he fed the ropes through the karabiners of his abseil anchors. He swore at the bloody woman for a fool, choking back his fear with the virulence of his oaths. He removed his gloves so that he could tie the ropes together tightly. He checked and double-checked the knot, the karabiners, and his harness. Exposed to the snow, his fingers quickly lost feeling again and he struggled to wrap the prussic knot neatly around the ropes. Long minutes later he put the gloves back on and was ready. He hated abseiling with all the revulsion of his deepest gut. It was the most dangerous thing a climber ever did. He hated Sophie for making him do it. He released the prussic and started his descent into the mist. The ropes fell away clear where he had thrown them. On such steep rock there was nothing for them to tangle on and in such still weather no wind to blow them off course. It took only minutes to descend what it had taken him so long to climb. The ledge appeared out of the mist. He called to Sophie as he came towards the end of the rope. Silence was his answer.

With his feet firmly on the ledge, he unclipped the ropes from his belay plate and called again.

Sophie, where are you?! The cry was almost high-pitched, squeaking through his throat.

The ledge was narrow and unclipped from the abseil ropes he was unprotected. He crouched down on the ledge on all fours. His first instinct, stronger even than looking for Sophie, was to make himself safe. He looked for her belay. The three wires were still where they had placed them, the karabiners lying forlornly against the rock, fringed with a lace of snow. He clipped into them. He took off his rucksack and clipped that into the belay too. He took out some chocolate from the pocket in the lid. It was harder than the rock so he thumped it against the wall to break it. He sat on his rucksack and gnawed the frozen candy and surveyed the ledge. Apart from the wires in the belay there was nothing to indicate that Sophie had ever been there.

The climber took stock. He was halfway up a huge north-facing wall. The Arctic summer seemed to be rapidly changing into Artic winter. His climbing partner had disappeared without trace. He wiped his nose on the back of hand. The snot froze on his glove. He tried to think of a reason why she would have untied and could think of none. But she had and she was not here and the ledge went nowhere. If Sophie was not on the ledge there was only one place that she could be and that was lying at the bottom of the cliff, probably dead, definitely seriously injured. The chocolate stuck to the roof of his mouth. He took a swig of icy water to clear it, and then he stood up and fed the end of the yellow rope through the karabiner of one of the wires and pulled the ropes down towards him. He was relieved when they came easily. He set up the next abseil, feeding the ropes down into the fog. This time it took him even longer to warm his fingers sufficiently to fiddle the ropes through the belay plate and to tie on the prussic loop. Failing in small things in their coldness and exhaustion and fear, climbers died, not killed by the mountain or the weather but by their own inattention to detail. Mountains did not deal in death he had told Sophie once. They only watched impassively as climbers committed the suicide of incompetence.

For the second time he lowered his weight onto the ropes and started his descent. This pitch was less steep and the ropes had not fallen as cleanly as before. He saw the red one snake out sideways where it must have caught on something. He swung towards it tugging it to him as he did so. It did not come. He pedalled his boots over rock slick with melting snow, following the red rope to the place where it was trapped. As he widened the angle of distance between himself and the abseil anchors the rope tension tried to pull him back. With his free hand he sought holds to aid his lateral movements. He noticed strange stains upon the rock, dark shapes where some mineral bled into the skin of granite. He saw one like a hand outstretched, clawing at the rock from the inside like a shadow-puppet climber clutching some vital inner hold. He took a deep breath. He would not allow his fear to play tricks upon him. All he had to do was free the red rope.

It was looped around a giant spike that loomed at him suddenly from the mist making him start and jerk away, his feet slipping on the damp rock. There was something menacing about the way it stood there silently holding his rope with its rough surface coruscated with carbuncles of rotting granite. The climber teetered towards it and tried to flick the rope free. The spike hung on tight. He swung nearer until he was close enough to touch the spike. As he did so something lodged behind it caught his eye, something absurdly bright in the swirling gloom. It was a fluorescent pink helmet. It was Sophie's helmet. He reached to pick it up. Sophie's blood-streaked face gazed back at him. It was not attached to her body.

He screamed and swung back behind the spike where he could not see what had just seen, what he hoped he had not seen, what he hoped was just a trick of the poor light and mist. He had steeled himself for a broken bloodied corpse but not this, not a disembodied head. He felt his eyes well with tears and heard himself whimper.

Please God let it be gone when I look again.

He looked again. It was still there. He could not bear to touch it but he forced himself to look at it properly, to look for clues. There were none. Just the head, strands of fair hair, stiff with rime, fringing the ludicrous pink helmet. She had called it her Girl Power helmet and he had rolled his eyes heavenward. Now its power to shock was as strong as the woman's frozen gaze. The head was Sophie's but it was not Sophie. He wanted to kick the foul thing down the cliff. But then he knew he would regret it later when he dreamed of Sophie's naked body in his arms, headless and bleeding.

He swung back behind the pinnacle to try to think what he should do. Human bodies were frail things in flight against the hardness of earth but he had not thought them this fragile that the force of an unimpeded fall could wrench a head from its body. He shuddered with something more than cold. However it had happened, Sophie was beyond his help. He had to get away from here.

Averting his eyes, he put one hand on the loop of red rope and the other on the top of the spike. The spike creaked and swayed. He tried to adjust his position. The hand on the rock stuck fast. With all the force of his terror he tried to pull it away but he could not lift it, could not break the grasp of the stone upon it. He put his other hand to it, to pull it away from the freezing rock, to break the hold of the rime that glued it there.

His heart missed a beat, and then raced away in panic. The rugosities of the stone seemed to seep over his fingers, encasing them in a granite glove. He pulled with his other hand but it too became fast. He kicked against the rock with his boots, trying to snap it, but its fragile rottenness had become fluid and plastic. Soon his boots, too, were becoming engulfed in liquid granite. Then the pain started in his fingers, hot and sharp and searing as if he had thrust them into acid.

For long minutes there was nothing but excruciating pain and the screams that it wrenched from his gut and heart and throat. He pulled and pushed and thrust and swore, twisting his body, arching his back, trying to break away. The more he struggled, the faster the rock flowed over him, searing with its liquid fire. The climber drove urgent force through his body, an arc of energy surging through his spine and pelvis. For a moment he clung there at the height of his spasm as if the snapping of his sinews would spring this deadly trap and spew him into the thin air of an honourable climber's death. Then he felt the final groan deep within and with it released the will to life. Legs and arms and torso encased in stone he was held in perfect stillness, embracing the unconsciousness that would release him from this terror, slipping silently into the engulfing rock. Beyond the freewill that had driven his life, beyond the superficial beauty of the mountains, beyond the fierce joy of working his body to its limits, beyond, at last, even the reptile cell-beat of survival, the climber slid into the stone and gave himself up to death.

The rock enclosed him to the neck, snapping off his head. It fell the full depth of the mountain to bounce at its foot hundreds of metres below. The cliff settled into a digestive torpor shrugging the female head after its companion. Human brains were too full of bitter strangeness for even a troll to dine upon.

HADDOCK AND CHICKPEAS

"Haddock and chickpeas, £2.99". That's what the blackboard said. Phil almost tripped over it in surprise, where it leant against the front of the Tithebarn pub on the corner of Station Street, its surreal message etched in multi-coloured chalk italics and forming a minor hazard to inattentive passers-by. He blinked and looked again. It was just a trick of that moody April sunshine, bright but shot through with patches of rain-sodden cloud. The kind of light that turned a scrawled "haddock, chips and peas" into something altogether more exotic. Phil turned up the collar of his cag against the sudden squall. Interesting combination, though, he thought, knowing nothing about cooking.

He went back to work. While his left brain was busy with the Council's accounts, his creative subconscious was enjoying a little exotic rebellion of its own.

"Why not try it" it whispered. "She might like it." Phil pushed the ledger away, tipped back onto the hind legs of his chair and gazed into the mysterious depths of his coffee. "Must wash this bloody mug" he muttered out loud. Inwardly, he said, "She might even be impressed". He flipped the chair back upright with a jauntiness that knocked a pile of invoices onto the floor. Bending down to retrieve them, he shouted under the desk to Cathy.

"Hey, Caz, you know where I can buy chickpeas?" Cathy was his source of advice on all issues domestic. She knew stuff that he could barely imagine. Like how to get Biro stains out of white shirts, and the right time of year to plant daffodil bulbs.

He had once brought his shrunken running vest into the office and pleaded with Cathy to perform some sort of miracle on it. "But, Caz, how was I to know that you're not supposed to put thermals in the hot cycle?" She'd been tempted, briefly, to offer to do his washing but had managed to choke the words back. "By reading the instructions on the label, Phil, like anybody else."

Now she didn't bother to ask why he had a sudden interest in alternative vegetables. Without looking up from her work, she shouted, "If you want to soak your own, go to the health food shop. If you want them in a tin, go to Sainsbury's."

Tinned sounded fine to Phil, so he went to the supermarket straight after work, having omitted to ask Cathy whether chickpeas were advisable on a first date.

It would be wrong to suggest that Angie was disappointed. Puzzled more like it. She stared at the plate and tried not exclaim "Gosh, an all-white meal. How very Conran!" Instead, she flicked open the paper napkin that Phil had stolen from his last pub-lunch and murmured an unconvincing "Looks good".

Phil wasn't at all sure about it. The rice was a mistake. Grilled white fish, dirty beige veg and bleached basmati. It did not look appetising. Anaemic maybe, but not appetising. Not that Phil was a much of a judge. Except for food items of the leafy and green variety, he favoured quantity over quality. Years of bivvying at the bottom of Alpine crags and eating in British transport caffs had reduced his criteria for judging food to the twin basics of calorific content and cheapness. When he and Jeff had come down from eight days on Ama Dablam they had tucked into sardine and chocolate chapattis without batting an eye-lid. In his poorer days, he had been known to scout around other people's leftovers, nicking their bacon rinds and fried egg-whites.

But even judged against his own low standards, the meal was awful. It hadn't even been cheap. He'd assumed that only smoked salmon and sturgeon were expensive and had nearly had apoplexy at the Sainsbury's fish counter when he'd found out how much two bits of haddock were going cost him. "It's the over-fishing, you see, love" explained the assistant. As he watched Angie pretend to tuck into the pallid meal, he regretted not ordering a take-away from the Balti.

The wine might still save the evening. It had cost nearly six quid and had a satisfyingly high alcohol count. Unfortunately it was red. When he produced it with a flourish, Angie had again to fight back her instant reaction, which went something along the lines of "Oh, what a shame you've haven't got a nice little Chardonnay. I was so much enjoying the white theme." This time there was the faintest hint of strain behind the smile that even Phil noticed. "Damn", he thought "I wouldn't have invited her if I'd known she was a wine snob." But he remembered how she had led the really steep pitch on "Phoenix" without any bother at all and decided he could overlook this slight flaw in her character. He did his wine-waiter impersonation and stood at her side to fill her glass.

"Would 'Modom' care to taste the wine?" he asked with a slight bow.

"Oh, just fill it up you soft bugger" came the reply. He poured a generous glassful and her hand did not come up to restrain him. Obviously she wasn't planning on driving anywhere tonight. Phil began to get his hopes up until he remembered that Angie lived within walking distance. He wasn't sure that a bleached dinner served with the wrong wine was going to be enough to persuade her to stay the night. But there was still dessert. All was not lost.

"It's just ice-cream for afters. Hope that's OK?"

"What kind?"

"Hagen Daz" There was an edge to his voice that almost screamed at her, please let this be the right answer. She gave him a real smile then.

"The best" she said. He sighed with relief and dashed into the kitchen to fetch it.

"How many balls? Er, I mean scoops. How many scoops would you like?"

"I generally find that two large ones are sufficient." Was she laughing at him? He didn't care. He was swept up in the energy of having done something right at last. Clattering the dishes onto the counter, flinging open the freezer, he snatched up the tub and ripped off the lid. He froze. He stared. He saw white. The pale, creamy white of vanilla-flavour ice-cream. Jesus! She would think he was some kind of clinical freak or a closet white supremacist. He would have to brazen it out.

He carried the dishes to the table with as much dignity as he could manage. As he placed Angie's in front of her, he said, "Try not to think of it as white. It's more a lighter shade of pale, really."

"I'll just think of it as Hagen Daz ice-cream, Phil, if that's OK."

When they'd finished, she offered to do the washing up. There was no way Phil wanted her in the kitchen. "No need. Why don't you just take your wine and have a more comfortable seat." He indicated the sofa with a nod of his head, hands full of dirty plates. "I'll just stack these on the draining board and the servants will do them later."

Angie ignored the sofa and strolled around the room, cradling her second glass of wine, peering at his photos. "Is this Ama Dablam? It's a fantastic mountain, isn't it? What route did you do?" Phil came to stand next to her and pointed out the line of the climb. It was so nice that she hadn't done what everyone else did and just asked outright "Did you get up it, then?" In reply to Angie's question he could tell the story, which was a good one, despite the lack of a summit photo. He even included the sardine and chocolate chapattis. She grinned. "Jamie Oliver, move over, here comes Phil Matthews, master of haute cuisine. Emphasis on the 'haute'."

He risked an arm laid briefly around her shoulders, turning her towards a different picture. She didn't flinch, but she did turn out of his arm to study the photo in more detail.

"I feel I should know where this is, but I can't place it."

"That's Crag X" he said. She turned her head to peer at him quizzically. There was slight flutter in Phil's stomach as he remembered her looking down at him from the main pitch of Phoenix, to tell him that she'd got a good piece of protection by the crux. Protection! He tried to remember if he had any. It was a while since he'd got a woman beyond the living room. Either they didn't fancy him or didn't fancy his house-keeping. Probably both. Just keep talking, he thought. So he talked climbing. More than that, he broke his pact with Jeff and told her about Crag X.

Lifting the photo off the wall, he showed her the line that they had been prospecting.

"I know it looks pretty shitty in the picture, but it's not that vegetated when you get to it. It's pretty steep though. And compact rock. Bit sparse in the runner department." He moved to the sofa and sat down, laying Crag X on the coffee table.

Angie perched on the arm, one leg cocked over the other, sipping her wine. "So when do you and Jeff intend to go for it?"

Phil sat back with a thud. "You haven't heard the news, then?"

"Uh huh. What news?"

"Jeff took a flier at the weekend. On the Ben. Off Smith's Route."

"Bloody hell, how is he?" She slid off the arm onto the sofa, genuinely concerned.

"Busted pelvis. I mean, he's lucky really, it could have been much worse." There was a second's pause. They both knew people for whom it had been much worse.

"What were conditions like? I'd heard that it'd been a really poor winter."

"Exactly. The bloody thing wasn't in condition. It was disintegrating. I don't know what the silly f★★ker was doing on it. I blame it on that Bruce Dickinson. Dick being the operative word. He must've persuaded him to do it. He wasn't the one on the sharp end when it happened though. He just got some rope burn." Phil got up to fetch the wine bottle. There wasn't much in it. He poured the dregs into Angie's glass.

"Here, finish this off." He went into the kitchen to get a beer, but kept on talking. "That's the trouble with Jeff. He's good, but he hasn't been climbing that long really. He still lets his enthusiasm get in the way of his judgement. He needs me around to keep him in order. I told him it was a waste of time going up to Scotland last weekend. I mean, for god's sake, look at how mild it was here."

Mild wasn't the word, thought Angie. It had been unseasonably hot. She had never before climbed on the grim fastness of East Buttress in early April.

"Is he going to be OK?"

Phil emerged from the kitchen with a bottle of Bud and sank back on the sofa, a little nearer to Angie than before.

"Oh, aye, I think so. He's still in Belford Hospital at the moment. But I've spoken to him on the phone. No head injuries, more's the pity. Might have banged some sense into his dim brain" He took a swig from the bottle snorting as the foam went up his nose. "But he won't be climbing for a bit". He put his arm back around her shoulders and bent her forward towards the photo. "So about this route…." he said.

Later, he wasn't sure whether the evening had been a success or not. He had managed to persuade her to try the climb with him the next day. In fact, she hadn't taken much persuading. Once he'd managed to convince her that Jeff wouldn't come after her to beat her up with his crutches, she'd jumped at the opportunity to put up a new route. Somewhere at the back of his mind, Phil knew that was why he was asking Angie and not one of the lads. Although Jeff would understand that they couldn't risk waiting till next year to bag the climb, he would still be pretty pissed off with Phil for doing it with someone else, after all the work they'd put into it together. But Phil thought he'd find it more difficult to be shitty about a woman. So that had been the ulterior motive in asking Angie for dinner. He'd had a vague hope that sex might have been included but he'd blown any chances in that regard once they'd agreed to go for the route next day. She'd removed the second beer from his hand and, to his horror, poured it down the sink.

"No more booze for you my lad. We need to be bright eyed and bushy tailed tomorrow."

He'd watched in a sort of daze as she'd grabbed her coat from the bottom of the banisters and given him a quick peck on the cheek. "Thanks for the meal, Phil. It was certainly unusual. See you in the morning. Eight o'clock sharp remember. The days are still on the short side. Sleep tight."

And Angie had been gone, just like that, walking quickly into the dark night, like a woman who had got what she came for.

When he arrived at the rendezvous next morning, Angie was already there. She offered to drive and he accepted gratefully. He'd had a bad night. He'd kept seeing that blank middle section of the climb, the one he and Jeff had cleaned with such diligence, the one with no apparent gear placements. He visualised the set of moves needed to get up it. They weren't easy, even in his imagination. And no amount of thinking made the cracks appear, those precious flaws in the rock where you could place bits of protection that would stop a fall. This was a climb that would probably kill you, if you fell off it. He'd proceeded to see himself do just that, hitting the ground with a crunch and waking up next to Jeff, both of them all plastered up and on drips, and with Jeff calling Phil a selfish bloody bastard who deserved all he got for reneging on their deal.

Phil settled into the passenger seat and closed his eyes, but his left hand clutched the door handle as if he was just waiting for an opportunity to throw himself out. Angie was miffed. She considered herself to be a reasonable driver and she was only doing fifty.

"Catching up on your zeds, Phil?"

"No, just trying to visualise myself climbing the bloody thing. It's a Johnny Dawes technique. Positive thinking. You see yourself climbing it exactly right and when you get to the top there's a pint of ale waiting for you."

Angie glanced at the door handle. Phil's knuckles were as white as last night's dinner.

"So talk me through it again. Just the one pitch, about 100 feet, with the crux in the middle?"

"Yeah" Phil kept his eyes closed. He actually didn't feel that well. Perhaps it was her driving. It certainly wasn't a hangover, since she'd so forcibly decanted his beer down the drain last night. Something that usually only happened after it had made at least a brief acquaintance with his stomach. The thought of throwing up made him want to. He screwed up his face and swallowed. Angie seemed oblivious to his suffering.

"You think it will go at about 5c?"

"Maybe easier. But there's no gear in the middle section. Maybe some stacked RPs. Might hold the weight of a falling mouse."

"You haven't tried pre-placing?"

Phil opened his eyes. "Shit no! We were going to place gear on the lead. Ethics and all that." As his stomach lurched, he began to wonder whether you could take this ethics lark too far. He was ready to concede that discretion could be the better part of valour after all.

"Of course, if you wanted, I suppose we could set up an abseil and place something at the crux."

"No we most certainly could not. I was only checking. If we're only talking 5b or 5c, when's the last time you fell off at that grade?"

"Oh, not since last night, actually. And then only a few times. Actually, Angie, do you think you could stop the car? I think I'm going to be sick."

She did and he was. Not violently, but he was glad it was out.

"Are you OK? Do you want to go back?"

"Naw, I'll be OK now. Just nerves."

And he did feel better. But not about the climb. That still scared the hell out of him.

At the parking spot, Angie checked again. "Are you sure you're feeling well enough? Do you want to do this?"

"Of course. I'm fine. I'm up for it as long as you are."

"Oh, I'm up for it alright." Energetic enthusiasm seeped from her every pore. Phil was jealous. This was his route, after all. Well, his and Jeff's.

"I guess you'll want to use your rack, Phil? How do you want to split it? Shall I take all the extenders, like last Saturday, and you take the rest of the stuff?"

"No need, I'll carry the whole thing. It's not far." Then he added, "No point in you tiring yourself out with a heavy pack. Keep your strength up for the route."

She gave him an odd look but she didn't argue. If some idiot wanted to prove his manhood by carrying all the gear, then that was fine by her.

The morning was gorgeous. Gorse glowed in the sun, and among the budding trees that grew along the beck, celandines studded the mossy carpet with their intense and joyful yellow. The air smelt fresh and warm. The rock would be dry. All was well with the world.

All was not well with Phil's stomach though. It had started to gurgle. There was something down there that it was not happy about. He got a shot of hot acid in his mouth. God, not again, he prayed, not in front of her, not again. The tide of nausea retreated.

They walked quickly over the springy turf, regarded with a sort of benign puzzlement by the sheep, whose constant chewing and mildly silly expressions made them look like a charabanc-full of daft old biddies sucking their dentures. Occasionally they remembered that they were sheep and sprang away from the human intruders, peeing themselves in abject fear.

Angie liked the Herdwicks. "I know there are too many of them, even after foot and mouth. I know it would be great to have more trees. But I've got a soft spot for them. They're as much a part of the landscape as the dry stone walls. It's all manmade anyway."

Except for the crags. They were not manmade and they rose up from the domesticated landscape as if holding themselves aloof from humans and all their works.

"There it is." Phil pointed to a small crag, almost buried in the hillside. It was not really surprising that no-one had bothered to climb there before.

"It's a bit small. Are you sure there's a hundred foot route there. And it's a bit green."

Phil put his hand on Angie's shoulder. It stopped him feeling dizzy. "Just wait till we're closer. Then you'll see the route."

Indeed, the crag did grow in scale and through the vegetation Angie saw the line of the route, a pale streak striking straight up through the slime and lichen.

"Bloody steep." she said. "Let's get a closer look."

They dumped their sacks at the base of the cleaned section. Before doing anything else, Angie slipped away to some boulders. Phil guessed she'd gone for a pee. He just turned his back and piddled on a juniper bush. Then there was a sudden contraction in his gut and he took himself off some distance.

When he came back, Angie was gearing up.

"I wouldn't go over there, if I were you" he announced, somewhat unnecessarily.

Angie didn't look up. She was fastening her harness. "Always good to shed some weight before a climb" she said, acknowledging that she'd got his meaning.

There was no discussion about who was going to lead this thing. It was his climb. That went without saying. Had he been here with Jeff there would have been wrangling, followed by a tossed coin. Today there was no debate.

As he sorted the gear onto his rack, Angie uncoiled the ropes, feeding first the red and then the blue into two neat piles at the bottom of the route. Then she looked for a belay. Although the bottom of the crag was flat and grassy she wanted to tie onto something. Phil was a good deal heavier than her and if he did come off there was a chance she would take off up the rock to join him. Unless there really were no runners, of course, in which case he would hit the deck beside her and her job would be to to call the rescue, probably telling them to bring a body-bag and a shovel with them.

Together, they studied the line. Slabby to start, then rising up steeply into a near vertical wall, before a large jagged crack led to an exit onto a broad ledge at the top. Angie was pleased to see that there was a small but stout tree growing on it.

"Is that tree good?"

"Yep, that's our abbing tree. Safe as houses." He hitched up his harness like John Wayne hitching his gun belt.

"Well, waddya say, L'ill Lady, how's about we give this here climb a try?"

She gave him that look again. "Sure, Duke, give it hell."

He chalked up his hands, and set off up the slab. It was easy to start, just padding up the rock, not much friction but enough little edges to give a secure footing. He fiddled in a small wire. It got steeper, but the edges were still there, showing cleanly where he and Jeff had knocked off the moss and lichen.

Probably an arrestable offence in a national park these days, he thought wryly. Another runner, a big one this time, a good rock on string.

"How's it going?" called Angie.

"Fine – falling elephant job, that one." He gave the runner a sharp tug. It was solid.

"Good, glad to hear it. How's it look ahead?"

"Steep".

The climbing was still on little flakes and edges, but now the rock was only a few degrees off the vertical. He placed his big toes on the footholds and trusted his weight to them, standing as relaxed as he could while he searched for some small flaw in the geology that would admit the placement of some protection. He cleaned out the back of a fine flakelet with his nut key, then jiggled with an RP until it sat, almost securely, but not quite. If he fell here, it would have to be very neatly and feet first. That would jam the miniscule metal wedge into place. Any acrobatics and it would just flip out. It looked several committing moves ahead, moving feet up to where his hands were, exchanging minute handhold for minute foothold, until reaching the bottom of the crack where it looked possible to rest and get some decently sized protection in. But not until then, not for 30 feet, at least. He took a deep breath.

To use the term "holds" to describe these small things that held him upright on the rock was a bit of an exaggeration. He could not actually hold onto them. They were what climbers optimistically called "positive". That is, he could place the tips of his fingers over them and stand on them with the very edge of his boots. These were not things he could grab hold of and swing up like a gibbon. What's more they were only effective together. Just one, even just two, would not be enough to support him. When he launched up to the next finger holds he had to be sure that his feet were going to make contact with the ones he'd just left. If they scrabbled onto nothing, all the finger strength in the world would not keep him on the rock. With his left hand on the more substantial hold above, he had to bring his right foot up high, his knee almost to his nose, until the front of his rubber shoe felt the flake beneath it. Then he sneaked his right arm upwards, curling the ends of three fingers around a sharp but very small edge. The words "Watch me here" sank heavily down the crag. Phil breathed out, straightened his spine and lifted his left leg high onto a small rugosity. He felt very precarious. He also felt sick.

He started breathing heavily, so rapid there was a danger that the movement of his chest might unbalance him. He needed gear and he needed it quick. Reluctantly he released the right-hand hold and reached down to his harness. He didn't dare turn to see what he was doing in case inclining his head toppled him off, nor could he tilt his hip to bring the gear closer towards him. He scrabbled among the dangling collection of equipment for the clip of tiny wires. There was a small crack to his right. He tried several combinations. Nothing seated properly. He stacked three pieces together, trusting none of them, clipping them into long extenders in case they lifted out as he climbed above them. He felt the rope tighten a bit. Angie was trying to give him a little more security, some tension on the rope to hold him in while he contemplated the next move. There was panic in his voice as he shouted "No! Keep it slack! This gear's crap, you'll pull it out!"

"Keep cool. I've got you and you know you can do this. Just go steady and head for the crack."

Phil was now feeling very ill. Usually, the focus of climbing drove out all other bodily sensations. Things like needing to pee, feeling hungry, even headaches were suppressed by the body in the overwhelming drive for survival. But this time that wasn't happening. Phil felt he was going to throw up and shit himself at the same time. Beads of sweat stood out on his brow. He felt cold. If this had happened down by that stonking runner he would have lowered off. Here he didn't have that choice. There was no way he could deliberately put his weight onto that teetering collection of cheese wires. He had to push on. If he died in the attempt, well, the way he felt that wouldn't be such a bad thing.

He swept his hand across the rock in the motion Jeff called the "window cleaner move." He'd thought he got this route taped, memorised where the key holds were, but that had been when he'd been functioning properly. Now his hand flailed over smooth rock, dusting it with chalk that glared whitely in the sun on the naked patches, where they'd removed the slime to reveal – what? To reveal holds that did not exist, that's what. In an agony of desperation, his fingers made a crease out of nothing, pinched on it, cranked, and suddenly his feet were running up the wall and his left hand was waving, and there was almost a hold, and then there wasn't and then his feet were running down the wall, and his right hand flew off and in a wild uncontrollable instinct he grabbed the little stack of wires and he felt each one ping, ping, ping out, but he didn't see them because he was already past them and, oh god, please don't let me flip over, the rope looping out in front of him, a yell, his, hers, both, a sudden yank in the small of his back and his left thigh, a slight bounce and he was hanging at the start of the steep section, with his left knee somewhere around his ear, looking with immense surprise at the dodgy RP now solidly, and probably permanently, welded into its crack.

A wave of unutterable relief swept through him to be rapidly followed by a flood of nausea.

"You OK, Phil?"

"Lower me down quick, I'm going to spew."

He managed to hang on until he hit the grass. Then without untying, he lay in a crumpled heap and threw his guts up. Within a nanosecond of stopping, he ripped off his harness, leaving it tied to the rope, and shot off behind the boulders. He was gone some time.

When he stumbled back, embarrassed to hell, Angie held out some water to him. "I think you'd better drink this." He sipped it tentatively, wondering whether it was going to stay where it was put, then lay back on the grass and closed his eyes.

"Are you going to die?"

"Actually I feel much better now."

"You said that after you threw up earlier."

"No I really mean it now. Whatever needed to get out is out."

"Mmm, so I noticed. Funny though, I don't remember you serving carrots and tomatoes with dinner last night."

"Careful, I don't feel better that much."

"Cold greasy tripe and raw eggs?"

"Bitch." He sat up, rubbing his leg. "No honestly, I really feel better. Like I could eat something even. Leg's a bit sore. Think I must have bruised it when I stopped."

"Here, let's have a look at it."

"Well, I think it's a groin strain, actually."

"In that case, you can examine it yourself. And have a chew on these." She tossed him a packet of glucose tablets. "You're obviously feeling better."

They ate some lunch, though Angie didn't let Phil have much despite his protestations.

"We both had the same last night and I feel OK. Did you forget to cook the other piece of fish or something?"

"Both under the grill for the same time."

"Rice reheated?"

"Fresh out of the boil-in-the-bag"

Angie rolled her eyes. She was going to have to show this guy that there was more to cooking than what you could heat over a camping stove.

"That leaves one thing then, and I do have a mate who has the same problem."

He looked at her.

"From the way you served them up, I take it you never cooked chickpeas before. Have you ever even eaten them before?"

"I thought so – in veggie curries, but maybe not."

"Well this other mate of mine is allergic to them. They have much the same effect on him as they seem to have had on you."

"Allergic to chickpeas?"

"Yup."

"Bugger."

"Whatever possessed you to serve plain chickpeas with fish in the first place?"

Phil didn't want to own up to the misread pub sign. She'd think he was illiterate as well as colour-blind, weak-stomached, and a slatternly housekeeper.

"I thought it might be different. Interesting, a bit exotic, like."

Angie screamed with laughter, holding her sides and literally rocking with amusement. Any moment he expected to see her wipe away the tears.

"Hilarious I'm sure. I was only trying my best."

Angie took some deep breaths. "I know you were, Phil, I'm sorry. It's just so bloody funny."

"It's not funny. I could have f★★king killed myself climbing in that state. And there's me criticising Jeff for going out when he shouldn't."

She leaned over and tapped him kindly on his bad leg. "You just need someone to look out for you, that's all." It was his turn to give her a funny look then, sort of wanting to laugh, but damned if he was going to be anything but deeply injured.

Angie looked at her watch. It was still only 12.30.

"Are you really feeling better?"

"Yes, really."

"Is the leg working OK?"

He stood up and walked around a bit, did a few desultory stretches. "Seems fine, just a bit of bruising I think."

Angie stood up. "Right then, we came to do this climb, so let's damn well do it. At least we know that one runner's good. As long as you don't mind belaying in a pool of your own sick, I know I won't hit the deck."

She was already over by the ropes, moving them away from the mess of partially digested chickpeas and transferring the gear from his harness to hers. He stood and stared.

"It's alright. It hardly smells at all. And if you feel a bit queasy again or your leg hurts I can always give a nice snug rope."

Silently he staggered over, exaggerating a slight limp, but unable to back out. He was thinking that Jeff would bloody kill him just as soon as he was sufficiently ambulant to do so. But that was at least six months off. In the meantime, if he whinged about the shock of his fall, his bruises, his food-poisoning, or the sheer terror he felt at the prospect of going back onto that horrible wall again, even on a top-rope, he knew that he wouldn't only lose this climb, he would lose any slight chance he might have with this woman. That was something, he suddenly realised, that bothered him. And then there was the fact that she knew about the secret crag. If they didn't do it now she would be on the phone tonight rounding up someone else to make an attempt on it tomorrow. Without him. So he put his harness back on, retied the rope and looked away from the congealing contents of his stomach.

She climbed quickly to the big runner, checked it, and turned round to give him the OK sign. That turn of the head again – it was something he noticed each time she did it. He found he was waiting for it as she got to the RP. She prodded, pulled and thumped at the tiny wire, changed the extender, but didn't turn to look down to him.

"It's welded" she shouted and climbed on. She moved confidently, balancing neatly on the small holds. Of course, she'd already seen him do it, he thought, and she wasn't allergic to chickpeas.

She paused where he had stacked the wires and tried herself. After several unhurried attempts to get something in place that she could trust, she put all the pieces back onto her harness. She had obviously decided not to bother. Angie climbed on with no protection. Also with no nausea, he thought bitterly, and no squits, and oh, with such supreme elegance. Where his feet had run up the wall like a cartoon character's, hers glided into position. Where he had done his impersonation of the demented window cleaner, she raised her arm, found the hold (my bloody chalk, though, seethed Phil), and closed her finger ends upon it tightly. She pushed away, gained height by the stretch of her left arm, up came the feet, balance, pause, inspect, no gear, move on, delicate, feather light moves, barely brushing the rock. He watched intently, feeling the space through the rope as the distance opened between Angie and that last runner. Time oozed slowly into the warm afternoon. Then with one more precarious balance move, she was at the crack. She braced herself across it and slipped in a middle-sized Friend. She was too high up for him to see the smile on her face, but he could hear it in her voice. "F★★king scary. F★★king fantastic."

After that, the crack was straightforward, with real holds and gear at acceptable intervals. She was soon on the ledge and putting a sling around the tree. Once she was safely tied on, she let out a war whoop.

"Well excavated, Phil. It's excellent. Now come on up."

He did his best. The moves still seemed hard to him, not because they weren't well within his usual climbing grade, but because when he got there, the fear came flooding back to him. He rather suspected that it always would, that he might never actually lead this route. He climbed it, with much scrabbling and swearing and with an unasked for, but silently accepted, tight rope.

When he flopped onto the ledge, Angie patted him on the back. "Just like a haddock – well, a climbing haddock, anyway."

"I'm glad you qualified that – I was just about to beat you to death with my flippers"

"Fins"

"Eh?"

"Haddock have fins. Seals have flippers."

"God, you're a bitch to a dying man."

"Yes, I know, it's great. What about the route though? Stonker, eh?"

"Yeah. Now I'm really scared about telling Jeff. If it'd been total crap it wouldn't seem so bad doing it without him."

"Well, I hope it wasn't bad doing it with me?"

Phil stopped in the middle of coiling his rope and looked her.

"Angie, I hope you don't expect an unprejudiced answer to

that question. I mean, the circumstances are what I'd call a tad complex."

"Fair enough, I can understand that. Did you and Jeff have a name planned?"

"We did. It's a bit spooky really, considering."

"Well?"

"You notice how the route is quite pale rock, where we cleaned it up? We were going to call it 'A Whiter Shade of Pale'."

"That's good. It means we're both working on the same theme. Because the name I'm going to give it relates to last night's dinner as well."

"The name *you're* going to give it?"

With the rope coiled and dropped over her shoulder, Angie stuck both thumbs down the front of her harness. "I did just lead it, didn't I?"

Phil looked at his feet, apparently absorbed in the task of removing his rock boots. "I 'spose so" he muttered.

"Then in honour of the unique circumstances, I give you the first ascent of "Haddock and Chickpeas."

They were still arguing about it as they walked out, back to the car, Angie striding ahead, Phil, weakened by the day's experiences, toiling along behind.

"But Angie, think about it, people are going to see that name and they're just going to know there's story behind it, and they're going to bloodywell ask and, frankly, it's f**king embarrassing, and I think you're just getting a cheap laugh at my expense."

"You've got to admit it's quite something. Not many routes start from a puddle of sicked-up chickpeas."

He was about to make an elaborately rude gesture behind her back, one that involved arms as well as fingers, but she turned to look at him over her shoulder and smiled.

"Phil, you must be starving. Why don't I cook you dinner?"

And he was netted. A climbing haddock caught and gaffed by a turn of the head. But, hopefully, not gutted. If she ever cooked him chickpeas, he'd know it was all over.

WALKING THE DOG

Emma had acquired Bongo in self-defence. It hadn't mattered when she was a runner. Then she'd just had to put up with inane comments of the "never mind, you're nearly there" and "he went thataway" variety. Of course, she'd also had to beat off one or two canines whose killer instincts were aroused by anything moving faster than their master's arthritic amble. But no-one had ever given her side-long glances, wordlessly questioning her right to be there. Pathways and parkways belonged to two varieties of human – joggers and people walking their dogs. And that was the point. You could run *without* a dog or walk *with* a dog. What you couldn't do was walk on your own, without canine accompaniment. So when the physio said she had to give up running or risk crippling her back permanently, Emma quit jogging and acquired the dog.

She described Bongo as a rescue mutt. Ostensibly, he was a black Labrador-Collie cross, about 4 years old and she knew nothing else about his history because neither did the RSPCA. He was an energetic animal with no discipline and was forever running off out of sight. She claimed that she got a friend to teach her a special whistle to call him back – she got a bit embarrassed shouting "Bongo!" in public spaces. Neither the call nor the whistle was effective. The other dog owners referred to him as Bongo the Invisible. Essentially Emma still walked on her own. But Bongo's lead held loosely in her hand was sufficient badge of belonging. People engaged her in brief conversation. She had reason to be there. The dog's lead and the occasional whistles made it all OK.

Emma had been on her own for a long time. She was used to it, though it never got any easier. People were suspicious of middle-aged women without families. Like walking in the park without a dog, it was against the natural order. At home she was protected by the reserve with which the British dignify their lack of curiosity. People were too polite to ask. But Emma holidayed in countries where families were big, boisterous and the very fabric of the community. Total strangers would ask how many children she had and how it was that her husband let her travel on her own. She learned early on not to say that she wasn't married. She could still hear the pity in the Pakistani woman's voice as she had put a sympathetic hand on her arm and said "Oh, I am so very sorry for you."

So these days she took precautions. Before each trip she would open the little box of treasures on the dressing table and take out the wedding ring. Always, always, there was a sharp pang of loss as she put it on her finger. She tried to remember, to imagine him putting it there, but it was so many years ago now, that she could no longer visualise his features. James had been her life, her one and only, own true love. Each time she was cross-examined by an inquisitive Sherpani or concerned Begum she had to swallow hard to fight back the tears. Maybe it was because these were the only occasions when she spoke about it, maybe that was why the words were so difficult to say. They would come out with a strangulated sob.

"Oh, my husband was killed in a climbing accident. Before we could start a family. No, no, it's OK, it was a long time ago. No, I've never wanted to remarry. I feel he's still here in these mountains somewhere, looking out for me. That's all I want." And the women would understand then, because a widow of substance was a woman with independence, a being allowed to have money, seek her own spirit and be herself.

Over the years, James had receded from the forefront of her mind. It had taken a long time, but now she could go through weeks on end without actively thinking of him. But he was always there in her heart, in her soul, in her body memory. He was the reason she was walking on her own, carrying a lead and shouting for a dog with a silly name. He was the reason she had no photographs of children to share with the Sherpanis.

James had been a keen and able mountaineer but not outstanding. He was one of those thousands of middle grade climbers who enjoy their sport quietly, away from the magazines and competitions and politics. He did some interesting and challenging stuff, but he never talked about it, never considered it or him to be anything special. So, in finding death in a particularly obscure range in western China, which hardly anyone had heard of, he managed to die as anonymously as he had lived. The incident did not make the news, and there were no obituaries in the climbing press. No body was recovered from the avalanche. To all intents and purposes, there was no record of his death, other than the empty space left in Emma's life.

Sometimes, after she had confessed her widowhood and lay down under a starlit Himalayan night, solitary in her tent, Emma would imagine James beside her, recalling how his body had felt next to hers as they cuddled close in their zip-together sleeping bags in some remote bivvy in the mountains. She remembered real conversations they had enjoyed and rehearsed the ones they had never had the time to have. And there were the climbs – all too few in reality, but in her longing encompassing the whole wide wilderness of the world. Then she would remember that he was no longer with her, that he would never be with her again, and she did not cry, but settled down to sleep, because she had been on her own so very long it now seemed natural. And she would wake up the next morning and breakfast with strangers but be among the mountains who were her friends and who would not leave her as her man had done. Back at home, she walked the dog.

She had just returned from a trip, when she went for a walk through a field she didn't go to very often. It was April and the lambs were leaping like toys on springs, charging around in gangs with their ears flattened into dinky handlebars, and head-butting their mothers. Emma loved to watch them. Their sheer joyfulness made her smile. Pity they would so quickly turn into sheep. Perhaps they knew their fate and that was why they packed each moment with such exuberance. It was like the passion that she and James had shared, the more intense and delightful for being so short-lived. Perhaps it would not have been so wonderful, after all, to have made old mutton in each other's company.

As always, Bongo was invisible and Emma strolled along swinging his lead against her side. She ignored the shout at first, not thinking that it was directed at her. But it came again, loud and angry. Her heart beat quickened. The shepherd was speeding towards her on his quad bike. There was no misunderstanding his words now.

"Get your bloody dog on a lead or I'll bloody shoot it."

Emma panicked, looking down stupidly at the lead in her hand.

"I'm sorry, I'm sorry. But, but…"

"You stupid woman. Do you know what a dog does to a lamb? You bloody off-comers. You're the ones who need shooting."

He stopped the bike and got off. He held a shotgun crooked over his arm. He meant business. What the hell was she to do? Should she tell him she didn't know where Bongo was, that he'd run off over the fell and that she was looking for him? Or that she'd had a senior moment and brought the dog out for a walk but forgotten the dog? Perhaps she could pretend to him that she carried the lead around with her just in case she found a missing trail hound that needed taking home. She glanced at the shepherd and then at the gun. Neither of them looked friendly.

"Well are you going to call the damn thing in or have you completely lost control of it?" He didn't actually say the words "you irresponsible cow" but they were definitely implied.

Shaking with emotion, Emma burst into tears. "I can't call him in, because he isn't there. My dog was killed in a car accident the other week. I'm just carrying the lead out of habit. I haven't got used to him not being there. I'm so sorry. It was stupid of me. I've lived here years. I know not to mix dogs and lambs. I do apologise for making it look like I had."

The shepherd looked doubtful, as if he thought he was being told a pack of lies. But he had to admit that he'd simply seen the woman with the lead and jumped to conclusions. He hadn't actually seen a dog on the loose and there was no sign of any distress among the sheep. He got back on the bike and turned the engine on.

"Well, missus, I'm sorry about your dog, but don't be so bloody daft in future." He drove off up the hill, wondering what these town folk had instead of brains.

Still shaken, Emma went straight home and made up the fire. She waited until there was a good blaze going, then poured herself a glass of wine. She laid the lead on the hearth. Gulping her drink, she went upstairs, picked up the treasure box and bore it down to the living room. She knelt by the fire, which was burning hot and strong. She threw the lead into the flames.

Then she opened the box. She picked up the wedding ring and laid it carefully to one side. It had been her grandmother's. She wanted to keep that. Underneath was a parcel of letters tied with ribbon. Undoing the bow, she picked up the top letter and opened it. She turned straight to the very end, to the words she fought so hard to forget, to erase from her memory.

"I wanted to love you. I think that I did for a while, very much. But when I see my kids, I know what true love is and that I can never really love you no matter how much we both try. I'm sorry to have hurt you, but this is goodbye. Please forget me and find someone who can make you happier than I ever could."

And there below it was James' signature, small, cramped and untidy, as if he had had to dash it off before his wife came into the room.

For a moment Emma's hand hovered over the other letters as if she might open them and reread all that impossible love. But she took another swig of wine and threw the whole lot on the fire where they burned away much more quickly than the lead of Bongo the non-existent dog.

MRS McTAGGART AND MARIA LUISA GO SHOPPING

The man behind the camera shuddered. What he saw through the lens was the dirty off-white of Scotland's deepest, most impenetrable clag. What he saw with his peripheral vision was his own hair, rigid with frost, like icy dreadlocks, poking out beneath the fleece sweatband. And that, he calculated, had been the fourth Big Mistake, the shopping spree of which the sweatband formed but a minor component part. He had been assured that it would make him look like a shit-hot Alpine skier, one with warm ears, a cool attitude, and a certain "je ne sais quoi". Instead it bunched his hair up into a nerdish ridge and rode up over his ears exposing them to almost certain frost-bite. The only thing about it that was cool, apart from his exposed flesh, was the price-tag. When he'd walked into Mountain Sport with a company credit card, he must have had "mug" written all over him. With only the merest swallow, he'd signed away the whole of the Arts Council grant. It was only when his "technical adviser", and his "actors" *and* the shop assistants all disappeared into the bar together that he began to wonder whether he'd been conned.

It wasn't even as if the stuff actually worked. He was standing on top of the highest mountain in Britain in the middle of what he'd learn to call a "white-out" wearing nigh on a grand's worth of gear and he was freezing cold. Not to mention just a teensy bit unnerved.

The fingers that held the camera had become numb. There was no sign of the "actors". He began to wonder whether they'd died down the gully or just buggered off for a cup of tea somewhere. He was certain that they'd lied to him about there being no café on the summit.

"Hey! Is there anybody out there?" His words sank into the dampness. He peered into the mist, looking for any sign of fellow humanity. A fat snowflake melted on his nose. He turned around, suddenly alarmed by the silence.

"Cindy! Where are you?" The quiet hiss of snow was all he got by way of answer.

"Bugger this, where the hell are you bastards?!" He supposed young Danny and Cameron were still down the gully hitting bits of ice with their picks and he hoped that Sid was catching the action on video. His so-called technical adviser, Allan, was probably with them just case the actors or the cameraman or the actual mountain itself needed rescuing. They hadn't been gone that long really. Not with all those ropes and slings and harnessy things to set up. No need to get paranoid. Except where the hell was Cindy? He'd been very doubtful about including her on the team in the first place. After all it was a lot to ask a city-girl to do, go stomping up Ben Nevis in the middle of winter with a clapperboard. By way of compensation, he'd shelled out for a particularly expensive pink fur hat that had taken her fancy in the shop. Probably much warmer than his headband. And now neither she, nor the clapperboard, was anywhere to be seen.

He glanced up at the whiteness above him. It was moving, fluttering down towards him in great white clumps. Just how long did it take for a human being to suffocate in snow, anyway? He tried to remember the Discovery Channel documentaries he'd watched as research for the project. He was fairly sure that you couldn't actually be avalanched on the *top* of a mountain. But he'd have preferred to have asked his climbers, just to make sure. Except they would probably have lied to him through barely concealed guffaws.

Big Mistake number one had been taking on this project in the first place. Fashion shoots, that was more his thing. Stick-thin models dressed in wisps of satin draped around antique statuary in some stately home in Essex. Not hairy-arsed mountaineers in Day-Glo Goretex dangling over precipices. Unfortunately, the public lapped it up, and the more severed ropes and mangled limbs there were the better. A guy had to make a living somehow. So he'd put himself in the capable hands of the Caledonian Mountaineering Club to supply the "actors" and of Western Highlands Mountain Rescue to supply the technical climbing and safety advice. Those had been Big Mistakes two and three, respectively.

He was getting colder. Shoving the viewfinder in a pocket, he began to jump up and down, and round and round, banging his torso with his arms. After less than a minute he stopped, knackered. "Probably the altitude", he thought. Perhaps he should search for the others. After all, it didn't look good for a director to misplace his entire crew on the first day. He took a step forward and watched as his ever-so-heavy and expensive plastic boot sank into the snow. He stopped. After due consideration lasting precisely a micro-second, he panicked. Which way was The Edge? In his mind, it was like that, with capitals, The Edge, not an Irish guitarist, but some fatal place where Death, also in upper case, was lurking to trap a poor innocent film-maker. He'd seen enough of those documentaries to know that it would be lingering and cold and horrible and, in his case, probably laughing at him in a Scottish accent.

But he hadn't expected it to be female.

"Are ye alright, Laddie?"

Still paralysed in mid-step, he felt a nervous flicker of fear at the top of his spine. He looked in the general direction of the voice. An old lady stepped out of the gloom, peering at him over rime-rimmed spectacles. He noticed the sensible tweed skirt and jacket, and then glanced at her feet. Yes, stout brogues and support stockings. Somehow he'd hoped the end would be more black-cloaked and skeletal. As a film-maker he was mildly disappointed.

"Only you look a wee bit cold. Would you like a drap o' sweet tay?"

"Tea?"

"Aye – I dinna hold with that coffee muck. Sweet tay's the thing on a day like this."

She put her shopping bag down in the snow. It was the normal plastic job with red lettering. He could see washing-up liquid and a carton of porridge oats. He looked again. It must have been a trick of the murky light. You couldn't walk across the summit plateau of the highest mountain in Britain with a Safeway's shopping bag. It was absolutely necessary to have a 75 litre high-altitude rucksack that cost at least £200. Without that you would die. Well, maybe Allan hadn't actually said that, but it had definitely been implied.

The old lady took a flask out of her bag, and poured tea into the lid. For a moment, the hot mist of steam rose to mingle with the cold mist of the impending blizzard. She pushed the mug at him.

"Here, Laddie, drink this. I think ye are going hypothermic."

In a daze, he wrapped his gloved hands around the mug and felt its warmth filter through his fingers. He sipped the tea. It was hot and sweet. He looked at her over the rim of the cup. She was smiling in a motherly sort of way, not really like a death rictus at all.

"Who are you? What are you doing up here?" He held the empty cup towards her and she refilled it.

"I could just as well ask the same of ye, but I suppose you're just one of those noodle-heads who chops their way up icy gullies for fun."

He threw the second cup down even faster than the first, feeling warmth begin to return to his hands and face.

"Er, no, not exactly. I'm making a film. About .....well about noodle-heads chopping their way up gullies for fun."

"Is that right? A film-maker? Are ye famous?"

"Richard Hankinson, maybe you've heard of me?"

The woman shook her head. "No, I dinna ken the name. Would it be Channel 4 you're working for? I dinna hold with Channel 4. Now that nice Mr. Connery, we had him filming here a few years ago, and my auld mather met Robert Donat when they were making The 39 Steps. You could say the McTaggarts are almost a motion-picture family. I've just bought myself one of these new VDU things. It's amazing, just like having a cinema in your own parlour. I thought I'd try this one tonight." She reached down into the bag and waved a DVD in front of Richard's face. In a blur, he saw a gladiator on the cover.

"So you see, Laddie, I know a thing or two about films, and I'm wondering where your crew is at."

Richard waved airily. "Oh they're filming in that gully over there. The one with the Mantrap in it. Or the Mousetrap. Or is it the Deathtrap, maybe? Yes, the Deathtrap, probably. In a gully. Somewhere."

She looked suspiciously in the direction of his flapping hand. "You're new to these mountains aren't ye, Mr. Hankinson?"

"Well, fashion videos are more my line, but I thought I'd branch out."

He was feeling much better now and remembered that he was a documentary film-maker with a job to do.

"Thank you very much for the tea, er, Mrs McTaggart, is it?"

"McTaggart, aye."

"And what brings you to the top of Ben Nevis in a blizzard exactly?"

"Just shopping, Laddie, just my weekly shopping."

He knew it, they had lied to him. Not only was there a café on top of the mountain, there was a branch of Safeways too.

"Thank heavens. I expect that's where Cindy's gone. That's my P.A., you understand. I, well, I sort of misplaced her. Temporarily. Probably went for coffee. Can you point me in the right direction?"

"Of what?"

"Of the shop, Mrs. McTaggart."

The woman indicated a general sort of down direction. "All the shops are in The Fort. Though you might be able to buy some tartan shortbread in Glen Nevis."

"You mean there isn't a shop up here?"

"Good heavens, Laddie, of course not. This is the summit of the highest mountain in Scotland. Who in their right minds would put a shop up here?"

Richard stared at Mrs. McTaggart, stared at the Safeway's bag. "You mean you've carried that bag of shopping all the way up from Fort William? Dressed like that?"

"Aye, of course. And how else should I be dressed on a dreech day like this? I'm not one of your half-naked fashion models."

Richard ran his hand down his face, a gesture hovering between frustration and bewilderment.

"But why?"

"Why what?"

"Why are you walking over the summit of the highest mountain in Britain in a blizzard with your shopping?"

"Because I live on the other side of it. And this is hardly a blizzard. Not yet anyway. And if you'll excuse me, Mr. Hankinson, I'd best be on my way."

She picked up her shopping and strode out into the gloom. He watched her go until she was just a blur and then he heard her words soaking through the fog.

"I hope your film crew come to fetch ye, Laddie."

Much to his surprise, "Death on Nevis" was a minor success. It played for several months on the Discovery Channel and was voted People's Choice at the Kendal Mountain Film Festival. Fortunately he was sporting his head band in order to look the part and so accepted the award without hearing the presenter's muffled aside about "the funniest climbing film since Vertical Limit." Indeed, as the memory of the shoot began to fade, he wondered whether it had been such a big mistake after all. Maybe it had been a canny career move. So when the offer came from National Geographic to do something on a slightly grander scale, he phoned Fort William. He got through to Allan first.

"Acancongua? Och, man, of course I know where it is. Leave it to me, I'll get the old team together. All expenses paid, you say? Danny and Cameron will definitely be up for the climbing. And I'm sure Cindy'd come on board."

"You're in contact with Cindy? I've been trying to get hold of her for months. Number unobtainable. She just seemed to disappear after "Nevis.""

"Mmm, well sort of.." Richard heard a hand going over the receiver and a muffled "Hey, Cindy, it's that Hankinson fella with another job." He could have sworn he heard giggles, but it was probably just crackles on the line. After all it was a long way from Essex to Lochaber.

So here he was on top of the highest mountain in South America. He'd been savvy this time, and refused to let his mountaineering colleagues take him shopping. He was still cold but at least he wasn't bankrupt. And this time he insisted that Allan was always with him. Although it wasn't snowing, a person could die on a mountain like this. It wasn't just a 4000 foot lump in Scotland after all.

He was just setting up the shot when he saw her. In fact she walked right into the frame.

"Hell's delight! I thought I told you to keep people off this section of the mountain!"

Allan coughed behind his hand. "Looks like a local, Boss. Not much we can do about them."

The woman wandered over and surveyed the two gringos curiously.

"Ola, senores. Mi llama Maria Luisa. Que se passe?"

"We are making a film" said Richard slowly, doing a passable charade of an old-fashioned movie camera at the same time. As this involved rotating his right hand close to his head, the woman's mistake was understandable. She looked at Allan and grinned.

"Es loco, no?"

"Si, es loco – mucho loco. Es Ingles."

Richard glared at Allan. "Don't think I didn't understand that!"

The mountaineer just smiled.

"Go on, Richard, ask her what she's doing on top of the highest mountain in South America wearing sandals made out of car tyres and carrying a basket."

Richard glanced at Maria Luisa and then at her basket. He regarded Allan with a certain narrowing of the eyes.

"I know that you are a professional mountaineer and Scotsman, whilst I am just a lowly film director from the south of England, but I know more about mountain people than you might think. They are hardy folk whose women think nothing of popping over the nearest summit to fetch the weekly supplies. Senorita Maria Luisa has been shopping, that's all. Now let's get this shot set up with Danny and Cameron. The rope cutting will be the pivotal scene."

THE BEAR

"F★★k! The bear!"

Stu sat bolt upright in his sleeping bag or as bolt upright as he could in a barely two-man tent. He elbowed Kev in the face in the process.

"God, you've got some sick fantasies" muttered Kev, having been forcibly released from his own by the application of Stu's elbow to his face.

"No" hissed Stu, "Not shag the bear. F★★k...." Pause for emphasis, "The Bear."

It was Kev's turn to sit up suddenly, nearly knocking his pee-bottle over in panic.

"You mean The Bear!" Like Stu he was talking in an exaggerated stage whisper, but the capital letters were clear enough to hear. "Where?"

"Outside." Kev rolled his eyes in irritation but the effect was lost in the pitch dark.

"Well, obviously, it's not inside, even I might have noticed."

"It's in the stores." Stu jabbed a finger in the direction of the stores dump. This gesture was also camouflaged by the darkness. He managed to stab Kev in the shoulder.

"How can you tell?"

"I can hear it."

Kev strained so hard he thought his ears might start to bleed with the altitude, but he couldn't hear anything except the wind. And they were both used to that by now.

"No, Stu, can't hear a thing."

"Well, I heard it. It was eating our sweets."

"Eating our sweets?! How do you know that?"

"I heard it unwrapping them."

"You heard The Bear unwrapping sweets? Bear as in large furry mammal with paws? Sweets as in things you can't get the bloody wrapping off with four fingers and an opposable thumb?!"

"Yeah".

Kev didn't have to see his mate's face to know that he was looking sheepish. He slid back down into his bag and buried his face into its baffles.

"For this, the man wakes me up from Lara Croft!" he growled into the down.

The next morning Kev was fetching water. He held the metal bottles and plastic water carriers neck-down into the floury looking stream, popping an iodine tablet into each filled receptacle. As he waited for the chemical to work he leant down to wash his face and something caught his eye. An indentation in the mud. Kev sat back on his haunches and looked at it. It looked suspiciously like something he did not want to see. He peered at it more closely to make sure. It was the pug-mark of a bear. And beside it was the cellophane wrapper of a barley sugar. Gingerly he picked this up between thumb and forefinger and slipped it into his jacket pocket. Best not to mention it to Stu, he reckoned. He stood up, making himself look as big as he could and scanned around. There was no sign of any other life, excepting Stu, and the term life could only be applied loosely to him before his first brew of the day. Kev walked a few metres along the stream. There were no other paw prints that he could see. Good. A one-legged bear was something they might handle. He returned to the bottles, gathered them up and ground his foot into the pug-mark.

The bear had first come to their attention a few days ago when they had run into a Dutch team breaking camp. The climbers had returned from several days on the Ogre where their summit attempt had been thwarted by the same storm that had curtailed the lads' route. They came back to a completely trashed campsite, equipment overturned, boxes ripped, tents and sleeping bags shredded. The animal had even managed to wrench the top off one of the plastic drums in which food was stored. Anything that wasn't in a tin had been eaten. The team was in danger of going severely hungry. Kev and Stu had given them some tea-bags and a bit of flour. But the lads were travelling unsupported, carrying all their food for the walk out to Hispar and didn't have much to spare.

"Well, look on the bright side" said Stu to the distraught Dutchmen. "You won't need many porters to ferry you out." Fortunately, the climbers were too exhausted by their failed attempt on the mountain to give Stu a thumping so an international incident had been avoided.

As there was little else they could do to help, Kev and Stu had reshouldered their heavy packs and plodded on. At the top of the pass they met the porters coming in to fetch the team from the Ogre. The Sirdar spoke good English, so the lads appraised him of the situation.

"Must've been a whole family of them" suggested Kev. "There's hardly anything left."

The Sirdar looked inscrutable through his fake Ray-Ban sunglasses. Kev noticed the label announcing their UV rating was still stuck to the lens, doubtless to increase their post-expedition resale value.

"Ah, no, Sahib. It is just one bear. We have seen him several times this season. Very old bear, I think, too old to make hunt." He grinned, giving a big display of broken teeth. "He like me – easier to eat your Western stuff than proper food!"

The lads had enjoyed the company of the porters for a night, bumming chapattis and goat meat in exchange for a few swigs from their highly illicit whisky bottle. They'd been saving it to celebrate their new route and when the storm had put pay to that, to mark Kev's 30th birthday, which was due to happen in a few days. Encouraged by the porters, they brought the festivities forward. Combined with the altitude, mal-nourishment and some weed thing that the Baltis chewed and which Stu felt compelled to try in the interests of his biology research, the alcohol had a stunning effect. Even Kev found himself trying to speak what he imagined was Balti, though it was more a mixture of sign-language with a smattering of Urdu and lots of English shouted at full volume in a "Days of the Raj" accent. Which was odd, given that Kevin came from Oldham.

As for Stu, he was dancing around the fire with the porters until he found himself holding hands with a big, hairy bandit of a man. He muttered something incomprehensible, to himself as well as his dancing partner, and stumbled off out of range of the firelight. And it was there, watching from the shadows, the golden flashes around its eyes looking like horn-rimmed spectacles, that Stu saw it. The Bear. Looking at him, Stuart Cameron, taking a leak. A feeling of immense vulnerability seeped its way through the narcotic fog. Stu rapidly returned his dick to his trousers.

"The bleeding thing's watching us" he stammered, falling onto the spare bit of carry-mat next to his mate.

"What is?" Gratefully, Kev broke off a particularly complicated conversation with one of the porters during which he had ascertained that the guy was an Ismaili, had one wife, five children, six goats and a second cousin in Rochdale.

"That bear, the one that wrecked the Dutch camp. It's out there, watching us. It's just waiting for one of us to get close enough and it'll f**king have us."

"Don't be daft. They're shy, these Himalayan bears. It won't be hanging around us lot with a fire going. It's just that stuff you've been chewing. Christ knows what it is."

"Well, I tell you Kev, I sobered up bloody quick when I saw it, and I swear it's there and it looked right back at me with those big eyes of his. I think it's fed up of egg powder and instant porridge. I think it's after easy meat."

Kev pinched his friend's arm through the layers of his duvet jacket. "Well, he won't get fat on what you've got to offer, youth." Their abortive efforts on the hill, carrying enormous loads, combined with the runs and a diet of dehydrated food had induced the kind of weight-loss that Doctor Atkins could only have dreamt about.

"Anyway" continued Kev, "These Himalayan bears are only little. We're not talking Grizzlies or Polar Bears, you know. Even if one was bold enough to attack a human, all you'd have to do is hit on the nose with your ski-pole."

"Hummm" commented Stu before he passed out.

That had been two days ago now and Stu's paranoia about the bear had begun to rub off on Kev. The expedition had been a disaster from the word go. To be the first fully grown human beings to be eaten by a Himalayan bear would just about put the tin lid on it. At least it would guarantee they'd get a mention in the climbing mags, thought Kev, morosely. As he watched the tea-water boiling, he fiddled with the sweet wrapper in his pocket.

Stu was still in his sleeping bag, lying with his head stuck out of the tent, waiting for Kev to stick a mug of sugary tea into his hand. He was finding it difficult to get motivated. They were still a couple of days of difficult walking from Hispar where they could get fresh food, and a long day's walk beyond that to the road-head where they might pick up a lift to Gilgit. Both men were knackered.

The trouble had started high up the mountain, when the ever-present wind had turned into an incessant howling gale. Until then, the trip had been a bit of a lark, nothing too serious, nothing that wasn't well within their capabilities, just a quick dash up an unclimbed hill under the cover of a trekking permit. The delays at the airport, the equipment that had been lost in transit until it mysteriously re-appeared in customs under the influence of a hefty bribe, the weevily rice and the cans of rancid butter, the terrifying drive to Skardu – in the beginning these were not indicators of potential disaster, they were just a normal part of climbing in the Karakoram. Kevin and Stuart soaked it all in, two lads on their holidays. They barely dared to dignify so slight an objective with the term expedition. All that had changed as they cowered in their snow hole, praying for the gale to stop.

It lasted for three days. The mountain had pitched and rolled in the maelstrom like a ship in full sail about to break its moorings and tear across the sky. They watched the white scourge of snow and ice-particles sweeping the slopes around them, insulated from the wind's roar by the walls of their cave. Their bivvy became a womb, nursing within it the two lives of Stuart Cameron and Kevin Postlethwaite. They eked out their fuel to melt snow to make tea and soup. Every so often one of them would prod open the door of the cave with an axe, clearing away the spindrift, keeping open their airway, their small window onto this white world. At first it was easy. They brewed, told stories, barracked each other and slept. By day two they were sharing fantasies, which actresses they fancied, how they were going to train their way to climbing E6, the first meal they were going eat when they got home. This one featured several times with many variations. Eventually they'd both agreed that they'd settle for any old actress as long as she would hold their ropes on The Bells, The Bells and treat them to a Big Jim Special at Pete's Eats afterwards.

By day three they were hungry, dehydrated and frightened. Kev admitted to the holes that were appearing in his marriage, Stu to the loneliness of his bachelor existence. Both knew that these were words that belonged only here in this self-contained shelter in the thin air of a storm-swept mountain. If the friends ever escaped this place, these confessions, slight though they were, would be left behind buried in the snow. As depression started to dig its dark claws into their brains, they spent most of the day dozing, their half-waking dreams being colourful and real and far more tangible than the featureless world of their white prison. Kev dreamt of Karon and the kids. Stu just dreamt about Karon.

On the morning of the fourth day, Kev stuck his head out of the hole and saw sunshine and blue sky. The snow sparkled in the still air as if the storm had never been. The lads crawled back down the mountain in silence. At their tent they consumed brews and calories until they fell asleep. The next morning they had struck camp without a word. The sun still shone and there was not a cloud in the sky but neither man broached the possibility of going back on the mountain. And now here they were, days later, no nearer home, and being stalked by a bear.

"Come on, Stu, shift your fat arse."

Stuart was shuffling around in his pit, trying to get dressed without exposing any of his skin to the cool morning air. He wormed one arm out to accept the mug that Kev held out to him.

"Bad night, I'm afraid. Kept hearing things."

"Yeah, so did I – you snoring, mainly."

Stu crawled a bit further forward so that he could crane his neck around the bell-end to look towards what they called their supply-dump. This was in fact a small plastic barrel. They took it in turns to strap it to their sacks.

"Any sign of damage?"

Kev looked up from his breakfast, working lumps of porridge out of his teeth with the end of a filthy finger.

"Didn't think to look," he lied. "How the hell can a bear work open a screw top?"

"He could slash it open."

"Sod it, Stu, it's just a Himalayan bear! It'll have claws like tooth-picks, not flaming razor wire."

He put his bowl down and reached forward to the drum. "But I'll check it, if that will make you get up."

One glance was enough to show the scratch-mark along its side. It hadn't ripped through but it had had a good go.

"Naw, nothing. You've just got this bloody bear on the brain." Kev stood up and started loading his rucksack.

Stu emerged sufficiently to start getting some breakfast. He watched his mate.

"What you putting that on your pack for, Kev? It's my turn with the barrel."

"Is it? Are you sure? Well, never mind, it's on now. I might as well carry it." He'd fixed it so the scratched bit was covered by the rucksack, out of sight. Of course, Stuart would see it eventually, but by then Kev would be able to blame the damage

65

on something else. A few days ago his reaction would have been to have come back from the stream shouting his head off about the paw mark, making absurdly exaggerated claims about its size. He would probably have enhanced the damage to the plastic drum by attacking it with his Swiss Army knife and teeth, just for the hilarious pleasure of seeing Stu's face in the few seconds before he realised he was being had. Now he couldn't see the funny side. Perhaps it was being nearly thirty. Maybe it took away your sense of humour.

Noon brought them to the first of the glacier crossings, the junction where the subsidiary glacier pushed its way into the main one. It was like a white-water rapid frozen in mid-surge, waves of ice thrown up into the air by the crushing pressure of one glacier grinding against the other. It looked impossible to cross safely. The lads exchanged dark looks and heavy sighs.

"Shit" said Stu, "Just when you thought it was safe to get back in the water."

"What do you reckon?"

"Well it's like that road sign says, the one outside Worcester."

"Eh?"

"Mingle and weave, man, mingle and weave."

"And that's the best advice you can come up with, you with your Single Pitch Climbing award and all?"

"Aye – and do it f★★king fast." With that he dived off into the sea of tottering pinnacles before Kev could stop him.

They threaded their way through seracs and rubble. The way was complex and, with Stu moving at a sort of gallop, they were frequently out of view of each other.

They had been going for about fifteen minutes when Kev caught sight of his mate's shadow against a wall of ice. Behind it he saw another, long, low and four-legged.

"Stu, Stu! Look out! The bear's behind you! The bloody thing's behind you!" He shouted obscenities at the top of his voice and banged his poles together. The shadows disappeared. Both of them. Silence except for the wind and the creaking of the ice-river. Kev felt a cold hand grip his heart and squeeze tight. Sod it! He had to see what was going on. He dropped his sack and took the hammer and axe from their loops. With no time to mess about finding and attaching crampons to his feet, he took two hefty swings with the tools at the top of a huge ice-block and launched himself onto its summit, feet flailing. It groaned under him. The surface was covered in the grit the glacier had accumulated on its descent down the mountain making it easy enough to stand. Kev surveyed the view, looking for his mate. He found him, trotting happily along. There was no sign of the bear. Kev shouted again.

"Stu! Are you OK?" With his voice sounding from above, unimpeded by the ice-towers, his words reached Stu, who stopped and turned around.

"What's up?"

"You OK?"

"Aye. Are you?"

Kev felt foolish. It had just been a trick of the light. Tiredness and hunger and anxiety were making him hallucinate.

"Yeah, Stu, I'm OK, just wanted to check where you were, that's all." He winced as Stu's laughter echoed off the ice-walls.

"Getting a wee bit frightened were we, Kev? Well, you ought to standing on that thing, it's going to collapse any minute. Why don't you come down like a good boy?"

Glad that his red face would be hidden beneath his sunburn, Kev turned around on his little plinth and wondered how the hell to get off it. While he contemplated his dilemma, he heard Stu shout "F**king hell, Kev! The bear's just below you. Just stay where you are. I'll scare it away."

"Hah, bloody, hah, you bastard" muttered Kev to himself. He could hear Stuart yelling fit to bust, screaming at him to stay on his ice tower, but he knew he was just taking the piss, so he whanged his ice-tools into the lip of the block and with a deep breath lowered himself off them, dropping the last few inches. As he struggled to get his pack back on, Stu came storming around the block, brandishing axes. He stopped when he saw that Kev was OK.

"You silly bastard f**ker! Why didn't you do what I told you. You were safe up there. The f**king thing could have bloody had you."

Kev gave Stuart an icy look. Sometimes his mate's heavy-handed sense of humour really pissed him off.

"And what f**king thing would that be, pray. Our friend the bear, perhaps? Now who's being neurotic?"

"Honestly, Kev, I'm not joking. I saw it. It was just lying in wait for you, waiting for you to step off the block."

"And you scared it away, eh?"

"Well, f**k you, you bastard, if you don't believe me. You can bloodywell look after yourself."

Stu strode away and was quickly out of sight. Highly irritated, Kev set off after him. Just around the block, he stopped. There was a small pile of fresh shit steaming gently on the ice. He was pretty sure it wasn't Stuart's.

That night, they camped in a pretty ablation valley, where a small cascade, fringed with red and yellow flowers created a back garden far superior to anything either of them had back home. Kev had an extensive and unruly jungle, which he occasionally entered under duress from Karon when she needed help with the heavier maintenance. Stuart quite liked gardening but his inner-city flat presented little scope beyond the window-sill. Once or twice he had been known to give Karon the hand that Kev couldn't quite manage.

However, they both admired this little display of exuberant nature. After days when the only colours they had seen were the greys and white of the glacier, the flowers assailed their senses like alcohol.

They were squatting on their sacks, rehydrating some kind of wall-paper paste that claimed on its label to be cod in parsley sauce.

"You know, Kev, much as I fancy Charlie Dimmock, I don't think she could do a water-feature as neat as that."

It was the first sentence either of them had uttered since the incident on the glacier that hadn't been of a purely practical nature.

Kev grinned. He didn't want to let the sun go down on their anger, either. Tempers flared when you were on expedition. It was one of those things. And it was all turning out to be much tougher than they'd anticipated. He remembered sitting in the pub, the night before they left, feeling brash with the beer, absolutely sure that they were going to cruise up their first ever peak in the Higher Ranges, and saying so, rather loudly.

Karon had put her hand on his arm. "Remember what Ted always used to say, and he'd done more Himalayan climbing than you two have had hot dinners."

"Ted, god I wish he was going with us, I owe everything I know about mountaineering to that old bugger."

"Well, remember his advice then – Come back, come back friends, come back having climbed the mountain. In that order.

The kids and I want you back, in one piece. And I want you and Stuart coming back still friends. I couldn't give a toss about you climbing the mountain, except that you'll be unbearable if you don't"

"He'll be bloody unbearable if he does, lass" said Stu who had overheard this exchange. "He'll have a head bigger than the bloody Ben!"

"Hey, everyone" called Kev, "Let's have a toast to Ted Smith. Absent Friends."

Now, in the fading light of a Karakoram evening, he looked at Stu.

"Here, pass us your plate, this gunge is about ready. Make the most of it, we could be back on solids by tomorrow."

"You reckon?"

"I think we could make Hispar by tomorrow night if we get an early start. Do you think you could manage that?"

Stuart stirred the fishy porridge on his plate.

"Aye, I reckon so. To get out of this place."

"You mean to get away from the bear, don't you?"

"So you believe me now, do you?" There was no aggression or resentment in Stuart's tone, just a sort of weariness.

"Thing is, Stu, I saw it tracking you. That's why I was up on that block, trying to warn you. It couldn't have been in two places at once."

"Well, I definitely saw it getting ready to ambush you. I saw it as clear as I did that night with the porters. And I know you think that was that drug thing, but I was stone-cold sober today and I still saw it."

Kev swallowed a mouthful of food and pulled a face.

"God, this is awful stuff. We have to make Hispar tomorrow. Just imagine freshly fried eggs and vegge curry." He paused. "Another thing Stu, you know when you thought you heard the bear last night."

"Eating sweets, aye, I know I'm an idiot."

"Maybe not. I found a pug-mark by the stream this morning and this.." He produced the cellophane wrapper from his pocket.

"Just litter" said Stu "One of us dropped it"

"That still doesn't explain the pug-mark. Or this." He got up and fetched the barrel, putting it down by Stuart's side.

Even in the half-light Stu could see the scratch. He ran his finger down it, where it had gouged the plastic.

"Bloody hell, Kev, why didn't you tell me this morning? Why did you pretend there was nothing wrong?"

Kev had wandered away from the tent and was standing by the waterfall, listening to its sweet gurgling, sounds that reminded him of his young son, Edward, not yet one year old, and of his two-year-old daughter, Tracey. He had his back to Stuart as he replied to him.

"I wondered that myself. You've been so paranoid, I thought maybe it would just make it worse, knowing there really was a bear around. But, you know, Stu, I've been thinking. That bear you saw by the porters' campfire and the one today on the glacier – that bear wasn't a real bear."

"What the hell do you mean? If it can make paw-prints and unwrap barley-sugars and gouge great chunks of plastic out of our barrel, I'd say it was pretty much real, wouldn't you?"

"Oh, there's a real bear around, I'll grant you. There was fresh bear scat on that glacier, I didn't imagine that."

Stu threw his empty plate onto the ground and revved up the stove to make tea. "So it's not all in my mind. Well, I'm relieved about that, I can tell you. There's enough going on in there already. No room for bloody bears, even wee ones."

"Exactly" said Kev. "We've both got minds full of all sort of shit. I know there are real bears around but The Bear, the one that's been stalking us, he's come out of all that stuff churning around in our heads, yours and mine."

"I never heard of a shared hallucination before and I've done some practical research, I can tell you."

Kev stared at the flowers. "Karon needs you, you know."

Stuart nearly knocked the pan off the stove and singed his fingers rescuing it. Kev laughed. "In the garden, I mean. I was thinking, perhaps the two of you could build me a water garden like this one."

"And what would you do, direct operations from a deck chair?"

"I'd just leave you to get on with it, mate."

Like I always have, he thought, though he hadn't realised it until they were locked in their snow hole, talking, and with the time to hear what was really being said between the lines of endless banter.

"She's really good your lass, you know" Stu had said, "You keep a tight hold on her, you lucky bastard." Of course it was the truth. Kev knew it was. Karon let him go his own way and asked for little in return.

"A good lass with a great ass" Stu had continued. It was then Kev realised that he had never once seen Stuart so much as pat Karon's bum or give her a goodnight kiss, outrageous Stuart who was all over his mates' wives and girlfriends and mothers, and yet had no woman of his own. And Karon who flirted with absolutely anybody she didn't really fancy. Karon, the mother of his children and Stuart, the best climbing partner he'd ever had.

Kev came back to the tent and accepted the mug of tea that Stuart handed him. He settled down on his rucksack, almost ready for bed. He suddenly remembered that today was his birthday. Thirty. It sounded horribly mature. A time to sort your life out and know what's really important to you sort of age. Scarier than a high altitude storm.

"I don't suppose there's any of that Scotch left, is there?"

"Aye, there's a wee dram – want a drop in your tea?"

"Yeah," said Kev, "That would be good. Sort of farewell to the mountain. This stuff'll be contraband again when we get to Hispar. Might as well finish it off."

Stu shared the last few drops between their mugs, then they clanked them together.

"Who to?" asked Stuart. "To Ted? He's the one to blame. It was his mountaineering tall stories got us both into all this in the first place."

He noticed that Kev was staring at the waterfall again.

"Or to Charlie Dimmock, maybe?"

"To The Bear. We can make him a den by that water garden you're going to build me. He's only little after all, and I don't think his claws are all that sharp. We can all learn to live with him, can't we?"

Stu had only the vaguest idea what his friend was on about but drank to it anyway.

THE SIZE OF WALES

Tufty stared into his brew.

"The thing is," he said, "Exactly how many whales?"

Bob stared at him.

"What do you mean, how many whales?"

"Well, you said, an ice-shelf the size of whales. So that would depend on how many whales and what species they were. Like are we talking about a couple of porpoises or maybe a couple of hundred giant Blues?"

Bob threw a piece of burnt toast at his mate's head.

"Wales the country, you steaming pillock, the place what we are sat in right now."

"Oh" said Tufty as the crust glanced off his temple. "I see."

Sid sauntered in from the kitchen, trying to peel a banana and drink a cup of tea simultaneously. He slid down onto the end of the bench with only a minor dribble of his brew. It puddled onto the wood alongside assorted other sticky patches.

"I've noticed that," he said. "Whenever there's any kind of environmental disaster, it's always the size of Wales. Bits dropping off glaciers, areas of Brazilian rainforest wiped out, that sort of thing."

"Unless it's in the States, then it's the size of Rhode Island."

"What's the point of that?"

"How d'you mean?"

"Who the hell knows what size is Rhode Island?"

"I suppose they do in America. Anyway, who knows what's the size of Wales?"

"Can I call a friend? It's a bit early in the morning for quizzes."

The lads looked up as Chrissy walked in, looking more cheerful than was strictly necessary on a wet morning in Snowdonia.

"Tea's in pot" said Sid "Fresh. Almost. Sleep OK?"

Chrissy pulled several mugs down from the shelf and peered into them critically before choosing one with slightly less engrained tannin deposits than the rest. "Yeah, slept fine, thanks. You guys?"

The lads exchanged glances.

"You mean you didn't hear it?"

"Tufty's snoring? I had ear plugs in. Slept like a baby."

"And that's another comparison I don't understand. Babies don't sleep. Believe me, I know." Sid shuddered at the thought of broken nights and nappy changes. "Then you come away on a climbing weekend to catch up on yer kip and that happens!"

"What happens? What've I missed?" Chrissy slid onto the bench and helped herself to a piece of Bob's toast.

"What brand are those ear-plugs of yours? I'm going to get some."

"Boots. Why?"

"Chrissy, my love, just go take a look at the front-door."

Armed with her mug of tea, Chrissy went out of the dining room and into the hall.

"Bloody hell!"

"I think she's noticed" muttered Tufty.

Chrissy came back in via the kitchen and topped up her tea.

"Think I need some sugar in it on account of the shock. Did I miss an axe-murderer or something?"

"Didn't need an axe, just used his fists."

"Must've hurt."

"Naw, I think he used his head. No pain in that."

"I still don't know what it is I slept through. Why exactly is there a very large hole in the front door?"

"Why d'you think?"

"I may not be Hercule Poirot, but at a wild guess, I'd say there was a fight."

The three blokes guffawed into their breakfasts.

"When he got hold of that kitchen knife I thought there was going to blood on the tracks, alright. Just as well Tufty managed to wrench it off him."

"Tufty?" Chrissy stared at him, aware that the tone of her voice probably impugned his manhood.

He grinned back at her over the rim of his mug and shrugged.

"Well, you know, needs must."

"It was GBH of the bloody lug 'ole, effin' and blindin'. Never heard the like. Much."

"Definitely not Marquis of Queensbury, that's for sure."

Chrissy had moseyed back into the kitchen. She pushed to one side last night's grill pan, covered in singed cheese, and started slicing fresh strawberries into yogurt.

"But who was it?"

"Some Beebs."

"Eh?"

"Birmingham Bouldering Club. It's their spot, after all."

"Yeah, their front door, even."

She stirred the fruit into the yogurt. Sid noticed that it was organic, fairly traded and expensive. He thought he was glad he was married to Susan, even if it did involve nappy changes.

"Come on, guys, tell me the whole story. It is raining, after all. It's not as if we're rushing off for a day of extreme Welsh cragging. I want to know what happened."

Bob pushed away the remains of his breakfast and leant forward on the table.

"Did you notice that lass in the pub last night?"

"Which? The pub was heaving."

"The gorgeous one in the white top, leaning on the bar."

"Not really, Bob, no."

"What he means" explained Sid, "is the woman with the big boobs and the white pully that had shrunk in the wash, and the big bum."

Bob scowled. "Not big, mate, beautifully proportioned."

Sid and Tufty grinned at each other. "He thinks she smiled at him, poor old sod."

"Well, anyway, it was her fault. As ever, if there's a fight between two blokes you can bet your last dollar there's a troublemaking woman at the bottom of it."

"The beautifully-proportioned bottom of it" added Sid with a wink.

Chrissy sniffed. "Mmmm. It's been my experience that if two blokes start swinging punches at each other, there's usually a very large quantity of alcohol at the bottom of it."

"There was" agreed Tufty "A very large quantity. An infinity even."

"But the Troublemaker was the fuel. Switched allegiance half way through the evening. Women!" Bob shot a glance at Chrissy. She just shovelled strawberries and yogurt into her mouth. Sid reached over her shoulder and poked at the contents of the bowl with his teaspoon. "What's that supposed to fuel, then? A day's flower-arranging?"

Chrissy swallowed and smiled. "Yeah, probably, knowing these Welsh crags. Snowdon lilies, most likely."

Bob wandered over to the window and stared at the rain. "What are we going to do, then?"

"I dunno. What do you suggest?"

"We could go and find a B&Q and buy a new door" suggested Tufty.

"Didn't notice you among the demolition party last night, Tuft."

"Yeah" agreed Bob. "I think the culprit will have to see to that, assuming he ever surfaces. I don't think I could be that drunk, now, and not die of alcohol poisoning in the night."

Sid patted him on the back.

"Terrible thing, age, i'nit?"

"What about the seacliffs?" asked Chrissy. "Weather might be better there"

Half an hour later, the four of them were stuffed into Bob's Honda Civic heading towards Anglesey. The rain ameliorated to mere drizzle. They parked the car at South Stack. The view out to sea was overcast but there was a bit of a breeze.

"What do you reckon?"

"It's gonna dry."

"C'mon then, let's give it a go."

They shouldered the sacks and set off through the heather. At the base of the upper cliff, they started to gear up. The heavens opened.

"Right on sodding cue!"

"Let's get a brew and sit it out."

"Sod that, let's go and find a pub."

"Guys, looks to me like this is just blowing in off the sea. Maybe we'd do better in the Moelwyns? Anyway, there's some easy stuff there that'll go in the wet."

"It's bloody miles to the Moelwyns! In the opposite bloody direction to the miles we've just driven! We don't have to go climbing you know. It's not obligatory. I can't stand climbing in the rain."

Chrissy punched Sid in the arm.

"Aw, Sidney, I thought you were so rufty-tufty."

"No, he's Tufty. But, yes, I'm very rufty as the lisping bishop said to the actress. It's what comes of climbing in the bloody wet."

Bob picked up his rucksack.

"It's my car and we're going to the Moelwyns. I'm not sitting around in a pub sipping fizzy water while you lot get stuck into a session."

By the time they got to Blaenau Ffestiniog a patch of blue sky was beginning to poke through the clouds. The air was damp but it wasn't actually raining.

"It's probably stopped on Anglesey as well, by now, we should just have had that brew in the café."

"Tufty, shut it. We're here now."

They pulled their rucksacks on again and set off along the track. The rock looked green and damp. No one said anything. Bob consulted the guidebook and wandered over to an area of rough rock, split by cracks.

"Easy classics" he announced.

Sid looked over his shoulder at Chrissy.

"Ready for that flower-arranging session?"

She reached out to touch a mossy patch of rock. Black slime oozed through her fingers.

"I'm not sure that I am, actually. This stuff looks a bit — well, primal."

"Bloody women! You were the one who wanted to climb in the rain."

"No I wasn't. I get scared climbing in the wet."

"You suggested this place!"

"Only because I thought it might be dry."

"Now then, kids, knock it off. Anyone would think you two were married."

"I am bloody married"

"I mean to each other, yer prat. Anyway, Tuft and I are going to do this route here." Bob had emptied his rucksack onto the squelching turf and was gearing up. Tufty glanced at the dripping crag. "Oh, right, I suppose we might as well. Since you're keen. Has it got any stars?"

"Three star classic."

Sid was squatted on a boulder with his head in his hands. "He means star*fish*."

Bob uncoiled his rope. It was yellow and exuded a sort of eerie glow in the grey light.

"Did you knick that rope from Sellafield?"

Bob smiled. "Nothing like a bit of radiation to dry out the rock."

"Well Chrissy, my lovely, we can slither our way up a wet crack or we can sit here and watch these two idiots frighten themselves silly."

The woman was staring past Sid's head. "Don't reckon we'll be doing either. Take a look at that." She pointed towards a huge, dark cloud spilling over the hillside.

By the time Bob and Tufty had got their kit back in their sacks everyone was sodden.

"There's always the climbing wall" said Chrissy helpfully.

"Oh, no, there bloody isn't" said Sid. "By the time we got there, we'd have spent over five hours in the car. We could have driven down to Pembroke for the afternoon. In fact, why don't we do that? We could set some kind of record for the number of Welsh crags visited in one day. Just as well it's such a minute bloody country."

"I climbed in Pembroke once" said Tufty. "It rained".

"Thanks for that, Tuft. That makes me feel a whole lot better. For this, I gave up a weekend of baby puke. Bob, take us back, before I begin to question my sanity."

Back at the hut they were greeted by a new front door. A young bloke was varnishing it. He looked pale. Bob grinned at him.

"Good bit of work, that. Specially with a headache."

Chrissy sidled past, keeping away from the wet varnish but trying to get a look at the lad's hands.

"There's not a mark on them, you know" she whispered to Sid when they got into the kitchen.

"No, it's like the hangovers, the scars don't show when you're that age."

Later they were all sat at the table eating dinner when an elderly man came in.

Bob half rose from the bench to shake hands. "Hi, Selwyn. How's it going?"

"Oh fine, fine." The newcomer nodded at the others.

"Selwyn's the caretaker for this place" explained Bob.

"You do a good job" said Chrissy. "It's the nicest hut I've ever stayed in."

"Yeah" said Sid. "It's even got a brand new door."

Selwyn looked over his shoulder, back through to the hall.

"That's what I thought. And I sort of thought that as I'm supposed to look after this place an'all, I'd better find out why."

"There was a bit of a fracas last night."

"I see."

"Oh, god, not us! Club members."

"That's alright then, I suppose. Do what they like in their own hut as long as they don't expect me to clear up after them. What exactly did they do to the door, then?"

"You know that young dark-haired lad, the one who's a shit-hot boulderer?"

"I wouldn't know about that. The club just pays me. I don't know them socially or anything. They all seem to be bits of kids, really. Anyway, I don't hold with this bouldering thing. It's not proper climbing, is it? Not like the old days." He sighed in a misty sort of way.

"Well, anyway," continued Bob, "there was a row about a girl, and me laddo took his frustration out on the door and punched a hole in it. I mean, really punched a hole in it."

Selwyn looked sceptical. "It was solid pine that door. Fitted it myself, I did."

"Well, it's true," said Chrissy. "I saw it. Big hole it was, like in a Tom and Jerry cartoon."

The caretaker was clearly unconvinced.

"Like how big, exactly?"

Tufty braced himself ready to dodge the assorted food missiles that were about to be launched at his head. "Oh", he said, "about the size of Wales."

THE FALL OF MARTIN PINCHER

The wind was the sound of silence, howling around mountains, making the deep-throated roar of emptiness. White was the colour of silence, its non-colour, the hue that absorbs all other light. Wind and whiteness, the mark of the mountain, making of the man who stood upon it, a thing of infinite smallness.

Martin Pincher bent to the gale and could not hear his heart or his breath above its howling. What he could not hear, he could feel, and these too were the sensations of silence and of a solitude almost too much to bear.

His hood was drawn tight around his face so that all he could see was a tunnelled view of snow and ice immediately in front. But he knew the emptiness was all around him and, at his back, the indifferent presence of the summit. Martin was going down.

He took a step, just one more in the trail of hundreds that lay between him and the mountain top; footprints that were filling with blown snow, obliterating his presence, leaving the mountain inviolate. He would descend to the camp and there would be no evidence that he had ever been here except for the precious images in his camera. He had to get down to prove what he had done, had to stand at the base of the mountain and look back up to its distant summit to know what and who he was. Without this mountain, Martin Pincher had no meaning.

So he took another step down. He lifted his foot, heavy with effort, and placed it a few inches in front of him. He leaned onto it, tensing the muscles in the thigh to take the strain. He breathed and felt the rasping cold of the air as it lined his throat with ice-crystals. He took one single step. The snow slid beneath his feet. For a moment he was suspended, a cartoon character, pedalling his feet against the empty air. Then it was if the mountain sprang above him, a white tiger rearing skywards. Suddenly, and briefly, he saw the summit and the pale sky and then the surreal sight of his own feet above him, crampons kicking their points into the clouds and failing to find purchase. And then he heard the other noise above the wind, the mortar-like crack as the snow burst away from the mountain and exploded all around him.

When he woke up he took a huge gulp of air sucking it in like a baby taking its first breath. His mouth filled with snow. He had the sensation that he was upside-down, standing on his head in a vat of concrete. He tried to think where his hands might be and located them across his chest, still clutching his ice-axe. He kicked his feet, iron-heavy but moving. Again he kicked and breathed and swallowed snow. He wriggled his arms, pushed his whole body in what he hoped was an upwards direction, stamped his boots against the encasing snow and felt them poke through into an area of no resistance. He pushed down with his arms, feeling his legs clear the snow as far as the knees. Martin pushed and writhed until he squirmed his way free, born again, feet first, somewhere on the mountain.

He lay on his back, panting mightily, too dehydrated to cry, too exhausted to scream. The hood had been torn from his face and when he dared to open his eyes he found himself staring at hard, bright, distant points of light. The air was still and very cold.

For the first time since the roaring of the storm had filled his head, he heard his own mind.

"Shit", he thought, "It's night."

He lifted one arm off the snow and then the other, followed by each leg. He felt no pain. Slowly he raised himself into a sitting position. Everything appeared to be working. With difficulty he wriggled the rucksack off his shoulders. He pinned it to the snow by sticking the ice-axe through one of the straps. His fingers refused to make the small, precise movements needed to squeeze open the buckle. Martin thrust his hands into his arm pits and rocked backwards and forwards on the snow. After long minutes of this a hot pain shot into his fingers. As he bit into his lip with the agony of returning blood, he tried to tell himself that this was a good thing. Being numb was bad. Being in pain meant that he was still alive. Once his fingers were working properly, he could get into the rucksack and find extra clothing and his torch and the tiny stove and make himself a hot drink. Beyond that, he could not think, did not need to think. Getting that far would be hard enough.

He scraped up snow into the little titanium pan, balanced it on the stove. It fell off. Martin lay down and stared at the stars. Then he sat up and refilled the pan and struggled to strike the petrol lighter with his gloved hands. A stream of expletives forced their way through cracked and swollen lips. Eventually a small blue flame appeared and he caught the gas and the stove revved into life. Martin lay down again and lost all focus amid the immense sky. Here, close to heaven and far from the light pollution of civilization, the Milky Way was a brilliant band of hard, glittering diamonds. Martin stared into their ancient light, knowing that he was looking at the past, huge, empty and unfathomable. The moon was a disk of ice, sliced from the glacier, its light striking sparkle from the snow. It was bright enough to show the shapes of the peaks all around him, as though the mountains simply spilled into the night sky to be continued there in the greater ranges of the galaxy, each star a summit that he would never climb and that would kill him if he tried. Space and mountains united in their silent and majestic emptiness, united in their hostility to man.

Martin wanted to cry but his eyes were too dry and sore. More than that, he wanted to sleep, but he knew he dare not until he had drunk and eaten and scraped some kind of shelter from the snow and wriggled himself into his bivvy sack. He forced himself to sit up again, searching through the contents of the rucksack for energy bars and drink powder. He ripped the wrapper off a Power Bar with his teeth and shoved the end of it into his mouth and sucked it, trying to soften it enough to chew. As he paused in his efforts to draw breath, he noticed the falling star.

Perhaps it was a planet. It was larger than the rest, its light slightly yellow, like a crude topaz accidentally set in a collar of brilliant-cut diamonds. It wavered against the night sky, getting gradually bigger, heading straight for Martin. He shoved the bar back in his mouth.

"It's a bloody meteor. I'm going to be hit by a meteor. Bugger." A sort of laugh formed in his chest though his throat was too tight to let it all out. He managed to bite a corner off the Power Bar. It tasted awful.

The meteor approached slowly, but, as Martin told himself, it was a bloody long way away. Maybe there was still enough time to drink a brew before it hit him and his tired body was pulped into the mountain. To be struck by a stray bit of extinct planet only hours after surviving an avalanche seemed unfair. The bright glow got bigger and filled his field of vision. He wasn't frightened, just resentful.

"At least let me have a last cup of tea before I die" he croaked.

"Jesus! Martin, you're alive. Thank God!"

Clearly it was a talking meteor. For some reason this did not surprise him. The fact that it addressed him by name seemed only just, considering what it was about to do to him. Its intense light struck him right across the face, made him reach up to protect his eyes with his arm. Then he felt the force of it, wrapping around his shoulders, pushing into his chest, and an insistent noise that sounded like "Oh, Martin, Martin, Martin, thank Christ, we thought we'd lost you." The voice reminded him of someone. "Diane" he croaked. "I love you. Marry me." Soft folds of down enfolded him, cocoon-like and he let his head slide into a lap. "Diane. Peter's gone. Up there. You can marry me now." And then the meteor was forcing hot liquid down his throat. It tasted just like tea.

The wind plucked a two-note, high-pitched whine from the guy-ropes and bent the domes of the tents obliquely into the mountain. Pemba and the cook boys, woolly hats pulled well down to meet the ratty collars of their old anoraks, skittered around the mess tent, adding rocks to the pegs as the structure leaned drunkenly before the gale.

The woman sat inside, huddled by the luxury of the gas stove. She held a paperback in front of her but did not look at it, her eyes focussed through the pages towards something far below, beneath the groundsheet, beneath the rocks, beneath the deep river of ice that was slowly carrying this mountain down to the sea, piece by piece.

"Ah, Mister Peter, Sahib! Hello!"

She heard Pemba's shout and dropped the book and ran out of the tent. A man staggered towards the camp, swayed and almost dropped into the Sherpa's arms. Instantly, one of the cook boys was there with the tea kettle and a plastic mug, pressing it into the hands of the climber. The woman threw her arms round Pete and hugged him, tea and rucksack and all.

"Thank god, you're back."

"Diane."

She looked into his eyes, tired and red. She didn't know which question to ask first.

"Where's Martin?"

Pete buried his face in her shoulder and wept.

"And the summit?"

The man shook his head.

"We never had a chance" he said.

THE PRECIOUS

The hobbit sat at the bottom of the crag, picking its feet. I dropped my sack downwind and nodded a terse acknowledgment. It grinned back at me.

"Hiya, Yoof" it said.

"Nice weather" I replied, not wanting to appear impolite.

"Aargh" it gargled "grand, eh but?"

My partner arrived, out of breath from the steep slog, and collapsed next to me.

I inclined my head towards the hobbit.

Sam lifted his face out of the turf and took a long look.

"That's who I think it is, isn't it".

I nodded. "Himself in the flesh".

"Not much of that" said Sam "He's even skinnier than his photos. Wraithlike, even."

"Wiry" I corrected.

"Oh, aye, wiry. I was forgetting you'd been on that diet."

He sat upright. His breathing had almost returned to normal.

"What are we doing then?"

I shoved the open book under his nose.

Sam took it, stared at the page, then stared at me.

"Mountain of Doom? Are you nuts?! I know you've shed some pounds, didn't realise it was all brain cells."

I snatched the book back. "Be alright" I muttered.

"There's no bloody gear in it." He stood up and looked up at the crag. "Nor no bloody holds, neither."

"I think we'd be OK." I fingered my new triple zero sized alien camming device, miniscule but perfectly formed. "I bought this specially. For the crux pitch."

"You *are* f**king nuts. That thing's so small you need a bloody microscope to see it. Wouldn't hold a falling leaf. Honest to god, Fred, lets have a do at something reasonable. Something just terrifying, not sodding suicidal."

I turned my back on him and put on my harness. "You don't have to lead any of it."

"Fred, it's a bloody traverse! With no gear. Including your precious alien. Doesn't matter which end of the rope I'm on. I'm not doing it." He was shouting quite loudly. Embarrassed, I was about to concede, when the hobbit called to me.

"Want to have a do at the Mountain, does ya, yoof?"

"Er, yes, I was thinking about it."

"Don't do to think about the Mountain of Doom. Aaargh, no, thinking about it does no good. Climbing it, that's what we likes."

I shrugged. "Well, it'll still be there another day."

"Aaargh, yoof, that's where you'd be wrong. No knowing if there'll *be* another day. Not if *they* have anything to do with it." He glanced quickly up at the sky as if looking for enemy aircraft. "And even if there is another day, no guaranteeing the route will still be around."

Sam stared at him and then back up at the route. "Loose is it, mate? As well as everything else that's wrong with it."

The hobbit hobbled across to us with bare feet and bowed legs. I had the strange vision of his knuckles dragging along the ground but I was sure it was just a trick of the light.

"Naw, nowt loose about the Mountain of Doom, but who knows, eh? I mean to say, who's to say, know what I mean?"

"Er, not exactly."

Thoughtfully the hobbit picked his nose, studied the result of these excavations, then chewed the end of his finger. "Thing is, *we* does know, you see." He leaned towards me and reached for my harness and ran his hand across the mass of gear hanging from it.

"Won't need any of this" he said. Then he gasped. His hand went to the triple zero. "Aaargh, except this. We likes this, we does."

"Bought it specially" I said.

"Best use it then, yoof. Bad luck to carry it around and not use it. *They* don't like it."

Sam rolled his eyes heavenward. "Yeah, well, I guess we can find somewhere to stuff it, to keep the climbing gods happy. C'mon, Fred, what are we doing? How about Riders of Rohan? Always fancied that. Three stars, low in the grade and good pro."

The hobbit suddenly straightened his bowed legs and jumped into the air. He landed right behind Sam and slid his hand over his shoulder.

"Not like Riders of Rohan. Nasty little route. Mountain of Doom is what we likes." He looked up at the huge cliff behind us. "That's why you brought it here."

Sam shrank away from his grip and looked at me.

"He's right, Sam." I said. "I did pay over fifty quid for the thing especially to climb this route."

"Well, that's fine. You just bloody go and do it. Me, I'm going for a few pints in the pub before I have to call the Rescue out. You've flipped your sodding lid."

Before I could stop him, he grabbed his rucksack and started back down the hill.

"And you're not the only one, either!" he shouted over his shoulder.

I watched him go, feeling abandoned and exhilarated at the same time. I touched the triple zero hanging at my waist and turned to grin at the hobbit.

I stuck out my hand. "Fred Bagshaw" I said.

He grabbed my fingers in his and I noticed how gnarled and knotted and clawlike they were. "Callum McGuffin" he replied. "We likes you, you're not like the others."

In a blur of activity, he sorted out both his rope and mine and before I even had him on belay was off up the first pitch. From what I'd read about him, I expected him to move steadily and smoothly, but he climbed in a sort of frenzy, almost springing between holds. What was even more amazing, he climbed bare foot and I swear I saw his toes coiling around the rock the same way that his fingers did. He didn't bother putting any protection in. I hoped this casual attitude to safety didn't run to his belaying technique. It seemed to take him less than ten minutes to run out the hundred foot pitch.

"C'mon, yoof!"

I followed him up the pitch, rather more slowly. Arriving at the stance I glanced across the wall of rock. It was steep, holdless and black. The route sneaked across, beneath a series of brutal overhangs. I felt a sort of squishy feeling in my stomach.

"There isn't much, is there?" I ventured.

"Aaaargh, it's the way of Doom Mountain. Nice climber lead the way."

I swallowed hard and wiped my hands on the back of my trousers. I decided that dipping in the chalk bag wasn't going to be enough and took the chalk ball out and applied it liberally to my hands and to the soles of my shoes.

"Is it as bad as it looks?"

He gave me a shove. "Must move fast. Must get to it before they do. Or nasty ones will take it."

I took my first step on minute flakes, took a second and knew that I had to keep moving. Nothing on this wall was substantial enough to stand on for more than a moment, so I made crablike progress as quickly as I could. After about a hundred feet I came to a tiny stance almost buried beneath an overhang. A raven was perched on the only place with sufficient room to stand. It looked at me and squawked malevolently.

"Bugger off" I said. It ignored me so I risked taking one hand off the rock to flap at it. It pecked my finger.

"You bloody bastard bird!" I yelled. I jabbed it with my nut-key and it hopped onto the arête just out of reach and fixed me with a beady eye.

I managed to fiddle in some bits of gear to make a half-decent belay and shouted for Callum to start climbing. He came across at a sort of loping gallop and I was hard pushed to take the rope in fast enough. The stance was tiny and he pressed his scrawny body against mine as he joined me. There was a terrible smell.

"Enjoy that did you, yoof?" Close up his breath was almost visible. My eyes watered.

"Bloody scary."

Callum laughed and I noticed for the first time how his broken teeth were all sort of sharp and pointed.

"That's nothing."

Without taking any of the redundant gear from me, he jumped onto the arête. The bird pecked his shin. Callum swooped down on it, grabbed it by the neck and bit its head off. He was near enough for me to hear the crunch. He turned to grin at me with black feathers sticking between his teeth. The squishy feeling in my stomach got worse. He threw the corpse down the cliff.

"We knew they'd be here, *waiting*."

Then he was around the arête with the rope paying out fast and I thought of Sam with a pint of Shires and felt a small but persistent whimper developing in my throat.

Far too quickly I got the call to climb. It was desperately hard. The rope snaked out to my left with not a runner on it. To fall here would be to swing across half the bloody cliff. It would probably mean death as I now considered it unlikely that my partner would have put any gear in the belay. I was a complete wreck when I got to him.

"Sam was right. I'm not good enough for this."

Callum gave me a bug-eyed stared.

"But you've got it. Nice climber have to do it." He stroked my arm. My silent whimper began to take on the dimensions of a scream. I fought it back and felt very sick. "We wants it. Nice climber have to get it. Before *they* do." A load of ravens, eight to be exact, skimmed in towards us croaking and squawking. They tried to dive bomb us, but we were crouched too tightly under the overhang.

I huddled into the rock as close I could and tried to ignore the fact that this more or less forced my face into McGuffin's groin.

"There's something weird going on here, mate." I muttered into his shorts.

"Nasty little birds. Won't let them hurt nice climber." With a high degree of alarm I felt his fingers running over my waist and along the harness. He stayed his hand by the triple zero. It was as if he wanted to touch it but that some force field around it stopped him. Worth every penny of fifty quid just for that, I thought.

"You go now, quickly, quickly. Aaaargh, can't hold them off for long."

Much as I wanted to leave this horrible stance with its demented birds and my even more demented climbing partner, I simply didn't feel that I was capable of leading the next pitch.

"It's no good Callum, mate, I'm not good enough. You'll have to do it."

"Nice climber has to do it. Nice climber has.." he paused and I felt the clawlike hand hovering on my harness again "....it!"

The dreadful smell, the incessant croaking, the churning in my stomach that had now crept down into my bowels competed with the certain belief that if I tried to lead the next pitch I would most assuredly die.

"OK, I'll do it" I said. "Where's this magic placement supposed to be then?"

"Aaaargh, it'll come to it. We knows that."

I took the guidebook out to check a source of information that wasn't suffering from advanced delusional psychosis. The page had gone blank. I flicked frantically. In front and behind there were perfectly normal route descriptions and the occasional marmite stain. But the description for Mountain of Doom had gone. There was nothing to be done except to step out from the ledge to my death. Anything was better than this nightmare.

It was a rising traverse. It got steeper and steeper until I found myself trying to claw my way up an overhanging rib of black, shiny rock on holds that were no bigger than a gnat's privates. The rock began to crumble under the force of my panicky grip. There was nothing between me and the belay except a huge swag of rope dropping down to a second who bit the heads off birds. I wondered what a two hundred foot leader fall would feel like and felt the last of my puny strength ebbing from my finger ends.

"Please, please, god," I sobbed "Just one runner placement, and I'll start believing in you I promise".

The miniscule crack appeared in front of my face. With appalling difficulty I held myself into the rock with my pinched finger ends and reached gently down to my harness for the Triple Zero. I pulled back the trigger and placed the tiny device into the crack. The cams expanded almost as if in slow motion. They bit firmly into the rock. I took a deep breath. They went on expanding and so did the sides of the crack. The stress of the camming was shattering the rock. I heard myself screaming and then I saw the white light come streaming out of the fissure. It got bigger and bigger and I heard the roar of falling rock and I was falling, down, down, down into the white light. The fall lasted a long time. Eons of rock sped past me, brilliantly illuminated. I stopped at last, bouncing on the rope and staring head first at what lay beneath me. It went quiet. I wondered if I was dead until I heard the all-too familiar voice.

"Aaaargh, yoof! Have you found it?"

I stared beneath me into the pulsating glowing light.

"Yes" I shouted "I believe I have."

I think it must have been much, much later that I woke up at the foot of the crag, strapped to a stretcher and with Sam hovering by my head.

"Bloody hell, Fred Bagshaw, you are one lucky bastard!"

"Am I all right?" I asked weakly.

"No you're not all right, but you're alive and you're here, thank god. Which is more than can be said for that sodding maniac you were climbing with."

"McGuffin? What's happened to him?"

"Dunno, disappeared down a bloody deep black hole, I hope. He wasn't on the other end of the rope when we found you, anyway."

Sam took my hand in his great big mitt and squeezed it. I whimpered slightly as a wave of pain shot up my arm.

"Fred Bagshaw, don't you ever pull a daft bugger trick like that ever again."

"But Sam, I found it."

"Found what?"

"I found it, Sam, I really did. The Triple Zero was the key, you see."

"Doctor! You told me to tell if he was confused. He's bloody raving!"

The mountain rescue doctor shone a torch in my eyes.

"Don't worry, lads, we'll have him in hospital soon. There's just a little matter of these coppers here. I've explained the seriousness of the patient's condition, but they want to question him immediately. They seem to think that he may have seen something."

I looked up from the stretcher and eight enormous ravens looked back.

ONCE UPON A MOUNTAIN

In the beginning there was the mountain. And because there was the mountain there was the valley, biting deep and rooting its remote heaven into the earth's core. And between the mountain and the valley there was the lake, cradled depth, window to the earth and mirror to the white majesty above. And because there was the mountain and the valley and the lake, there was everything that ever was upon the earth and beneath the sky.

The woman looked and saw the mountain and felt the churning of her guts and the breaking of her heart, reliving those sensations in the memory of her body, remembering how a landscape had punched a hole into her chest to let the awe flow in and the love flow out. She felt the dampness welling in her eyes and caught her breath in a choking cough.

"They're beautiful" she said, dropping the magazine onto the bed. Her hand stayed flat upon the biggest photograph, covering the mountain with her palm as if to absorb it into her body. She looked at the man sat by the bed and smiled. "Thanks for bringing them to show me."

He reached across the covers and slid the magazine from under her hand. He scanned the photograph as if seeing it for the first time. "You don't mind, do you?"

"Whyever should I mind?"

"I didn't know if you'd be upset. Not just the pictures, the article. I was worried you would find it painful."

The woman winced. She struggled against the pillows to change her position.

"Could you...?"

"Where do you want to be?"

"Sit me more upright please."

The man stood up and reached under her arms, then stopped. She laughed.

"It's alright, you know. I don't bite, not anymore." And he bent down to her and lifted her small weight in his hands and settled her against the too-white, too crisp pillows. She smiled her thank you and he sat back in the chair and rolled the magazine in his hands.

"Mike." He stopped fiddling but did not look at her.

"Of course I find it painful."

"I'm sorry, I shouldn't have come."

"Don't be a plonker, Mike. I mean my body hurts. Hurts like buggery, sometimes. And being in here, that isn't exactly a barrel of laughs, either." She nodded her head towards the cupboard. "Can you get me some OJ please?"

He went to the cupboard and shook the carton and poured juice into the plastic glass and put it in her hand. He surveyed the room, taking in the flowers and cards, along with the tubes and the white walls and the nauseating smell of disinfectant.

"Have they said how long you'll have to stay here?"

"No, not yet. They think I might need another operation."

"And will that one work?"

She pushed the empty glass towards him and he took it and set it on the bedside table without looking at it, without taking his eyes away from her.

"They won't know until they try it."

"Like us and the mountain then?"

"Yes. Like us and other things, too."

Mike got up out of the chair and looked out of the window.

"I wish I could do that," she said.

"Jesus, Sally, I'm sorry. There's nothing I can say, is there?"

"You can tell me what you can see out of the window."

He turned his head towards her.

"You mean you don't even know what's out of the window?"

"No, I haven't bothered the nurses. They've got enough to do taking me to the loo. At least I can wipe my own arse."

"It's difficult to get my head around what's happened."

"I thought that was what the article was about. Catharsis. Or something."

He thwacked the rolled up magazine against the window sill.

"Bloody article. Wish I hadn't written it."

"I hope they paid you."

"Sally, don't be angry. If I hadn't done it someone else would've. And got it wrong. You know what they're like."

She smiled at his back. "And your pictures are better. So tell me what you can see out of the window."

"Are you sure you want to know?"

"Of course. What is it, the bloody morgue?"

"It's a concrete wall, with some wheelie bins."

"No wonder they use this room for the spazzes."

Mike turned angrily. "Don't say that, Sally."

"What? Call myself a spaz? What else would you call me?"

"You're still you, Sally. And you're going to get better. You'll be walking again soon, for sure. I know you."

"Perhaps you should write the book, Mike. Triumph and Tragedy in Tibet. Or something. How you dug me out of the avalanche with your bare hands and carried me down the mountain."

"I'd rather write about the way you forced a route up that last ice-field."

"So would I, actually. But it's the tragedy bit that sells."

Mike moved across the room to the shelf above the radiator. He picked up a card and looked at it.

"A lot of people care about you, you know."

"Yes, I do know. Amazing how nearly getting killed brings your mates out of the woodwork."

"They weren't *in* the woodwork, Sally."

"You're right. I'm sorry. I'm just at the self-pity stage. I guess I'll work through it."

"Sal – you'll have this other operation. It'll be O.K. If anybody can beat this thing, you can. God knows, you're a tough bloody cow, you'll be back on the crags next summer."

"Climbing with you, Mike?"

He picked up another card and stared at it.

"Don't let that get in the way, Sal."

"Pass me that box of tissues, please."

"Please don't cry."

"I'm not going to bloody cry. I need to blow my nose. Git."

He passed the box to her and sat back on the edge of the bed.

"Have they said when this operation might be?"

"Not yet. I don't know."

"Only I'd like to know before I go."

Sally sniffed into a tissue.

"We could try asking the orderly when he comes round with the tea, but I don't think he'll know."

"I don't mean before I go this afternoon. I mean before I go to South America."

She stared at him.

"South America? When are you going there?"

"Next month. I've been invited to join Dave Johnson's trip."

"*The* Dave Johnson?"

Mike nodded.

"Playing with the big boys, Mike. That's an honour."

He shrugged. "Well, you know, what we did in Tibet. It was a bit of an achievement."

"Yes, it was – especially that final ice-field."

He touched the back of her hand.

"I'm sure Dave would have rather had you along than me. I'm sure I'm just second best."

"Be careful. Don't go cutting any ropes."

He smiled and squeezed her hand. "I'll try not too. That plot line's been used up."

"How long will you be away?"

"Couple of months maybe. I'm leaving it open. See how things go. Might do some travelling while I'm out there. Go down to Patagonia, maybe."

"Right." Her fingers started to intertwine with his and he slid his hand away.

"You'll be climbing again by the time I'm back."

"You always were a bloody useless liar."

"What do you mean?"

"If you thought I'd be climbing in three months time or even in a year's time, you wouldn't be going."

He stood up and walked back to the window.

"They'll be here with my tea soon. They'll ask you sit outside while I gag my way through it."

"I'd better not wait. Got some things I need to do."

"S'pose you've got a lot on, getting ready for the trip."

"I just wanted you to see the article."

"Anyone could've shown me the bloody article."

"*I* wanted to show you the article. I wanted to see you."

"Before you go."

"Before I go. I wanted to say sorry."

Sally shrugged. "You saved my life. That's pretty good as apologies go. Guess I'll make do with that."

There was silence for several minutes. Sally fiddled with the tissues and Mike picked up the magazine again and flicked through the pages. She coughed.

"Mike?"

"Yeah?"

"It wasn't worth it."

"What wasn't?"

"The f**king, bloody mountain. It wasn't worth this." She banged her fist into her legs. "And it wasn't worth this either, you bastard." She threw the box of tissues at his head and missed.

"I think I'd better go."

"Yes, walk out. *You* can."

He didn't move. Again there was silence.

"Mike? Tell me what you can see out of the window. Not the wheelie bins."

He settled his hands on the window sill and stared out at the concrete wall.

"I see the most beautiful mountain in the world. It's got fabulous ridges sweeping up to a really pointy summit. It's all sparkly white against a blue sky. Dark blue, not a cloud to be seen. Below it there's a green valley and a lake shimmering in the sunshine."

"Are there any people?"

"Yes, a man and a woman."

"Are they climbing the mountain?"

"No, they've already summited. They're in their tent."

"Brewing up?"

"Celebrating."

"How?"

"Humping the living daylights out of each other."

"You always were a romantic bastard."

He turned back to her and smiled. "Try to be. Not good at it, though, am I?"

"Humping sounds good to me. Brings back fond memories. Like climbing and going for a pee under my own steam."

Mike looked at the floor. "I wish we'd never gone there, Sal, but we did. I wish I could cope with all this, but I can't. I'm a git and a bastard. I'm sorry."

"I f**king know that."

The door opened.

"Hiya, Sally, tea time!" The orderly pushed his way in behind a rattling trolley. "Sorry, sir, but there's no visitors while patients are eating. Hygiene regs."

"It's O.K. I'm going anyway."

"You can wait in the day room till she's finished if you want. I think they're watching "Countdown" on the telly."

"Thanks, but it's O.K."

Mike came back to the bed and brushed Sally's hand.

"I'll leave you the mag."

"Thanks. And thanks for coming I suppose. I know you don't usually do sick visits."

Mike looked at the trolley as he moved past.

"Looks better than hillfood, anyway."

"Yeah, just about. Send me a postcard."

Mike smiled. "Yeah, loads." He waved and went out and closed the door behind him and Sally let herself sink beneath the inane chatter of the orderly.

In the end there would be just the photograph of a mountain in an old climbing magazine. Because of the mountain there was nothing else left.

THE GREAT WALDO PEPPER

When I first met Voodoo at the cliff I can remember exactly what I said. I went right up to her and said, "Call me Pepper," that's what I said. And she said,

"Like you mean, as in Doctor Pepper?"

And I said "No way. As in, like, my colouring, you know. Salt and…?"

And she gave me a kinda knowing look with her head on one side and said, "Oh, that's what *they* call you I guess. No worries. It's kinda cute. Sure. Hiya Pepper, how's it goin'?"

Well, she was some bitch that Voodoo. She played it cool alright but I could smell them pheromones rising off a her like steam off a potroast on a hot day. I sauntered right over to the bottom of the hardest route around. Ben was already there, eying it up, kinda rehearsing the moves. He'd stripped down to his shorts and was practising his "arm-bar lock-offs" for the benefit of Voodoo's friend, Mary Lou. Those moves didn't work for shit on the rock, but they were pretty damn good at showing off his way-honed muscles. Then he did a long bend and stretch so that she could get a good look at his butt.

The girl laughed.

"Hey, Voodoo, will ya look at that? Don't it make ya come over all fragile?" Voodoo did look, so I took my chance and pee-ed all over the sitting start. That'll impress the bitch, I thought.

"Hey, Ben" the girl called over. "Looks like Pepper don't think it's hard enough for ya." Ben had been too busy doing backbends to notice but when she pointed it out he was obliged to look. He whipped off his baseball cap and hit me around the head with it. "Dammit, Pepper, I ain't ever gonna bring you out climbing again, I swear!"

I knew Voodoo was watching, so I got a-hold a the cap in my teeth. Ben pulled and I pulled, and there wasn't either one of us gonna give way. But the cap did. Ben found it bleaching on a rock on a hike we made though Canyonlands at least five years before, so it wasn't hardly surprising.

We got half each.

The girl winked at Voodoo.

"Let's show the guys some proper team work shall we, babe?" She set off up her route, climbing quickly. It was a full rope length to the top of the outcrop, but she was still up it before Ben had even finished his warm-ups. She took the rope in and Voodoo set off after her. God, but it was something to behold. That bitch could climb and then some.

I looked at Ben. He shrugged.

"Vertical walkies. Huh!" With a final flex of his pecs he lay down under the rock, stuck a leg in the air and heel-hooked a micro-flake. Pushing off a the ground with one hand, he pinched a crystal with the other and levered himself upwards. He then proceeded to execute the complete boulder problem upside down. I reckon it was meant to impress but I heard the girl laugh from the top of her rock and Voodoo just howled. Hanging upside down from bum holds, Ben couldn't make the finishing moves onto the top of the boulder and dropped off onto the bouldering mat head first. I had to skip off sideways pretty goddamn sharp. It's difficult to impress a female from the squished position.

The girls came back down. Mary Lou poked Ben in the ribs with her toe.

"You OK?"

Ben rubbed his neck. "I'll live."

Voodoo was sniffing around me like she was interested but definitely not convinced. "You climb at all, Pepper?" She said it kinda cool like she meant it straight up but from the look in her eye I knew what she meant was "or do you just wait at the bottom watching *him?*"

I wasn't having that so I skirted around behind her to get a clear run at her butt. Voodoo was too quick for me and jumped right around and snarled fiercer than a grizzly bear with hives. I knew I wasn't gonna win this babe just on Jack Russell charm and personality. I squared my shoulders. "Me and Ben just boulder. No ropes, no runners. Pure climbing. Just man, dog and rock."

She cocked her head on one side.

"So show me."

Well, I'd seen enough of Voodoo's tail to scramble my brains alright. I took a short run and made one godalmighty leap up the problem Ben had just crashed off of. I made brief contact with the rock, enough to scrabble a few inches higher, got a claw in a crack, scratched for all I was worth, powered with my back legs, smeared with my front paws and sprang for the top of the boulder. I got real high and thought I'd land square on top of the damned thing, but when I hit rock I only had one hind leg in contact and I span and flipped and the next thing I know I'm doing a double somersault through fresh air. First I see the trees, then the ground, then the trees again. Uh huh, I thought, this ain't too good. I kinda twisted myself around in mid flight so I could land paws first. It musta looked pretty spectacular. Afterwards Ben called it my Triple Salko with Double Toe-

Loop. Given the effect it had on Voodoo, I prefer to think of it as my Victory Roll. I crashed right down onto the mat in front of all three of 'em. Couldn't have done it better if I'd a rehearsed it.

"Jeez, Pepper, you OK?" Ben tried to pick me up, but I gave him my "back-off, human" curl of the lip. I didn't want no fussing to spoil the effect. What did he think I was, some kinda pooch?

"Oh, Ben, he's fine" said Mary Lou, "In fact, I'd swear to god, he's grinning from ear to ear."

Voodoo jumped onto the mat and licked my face, tail wagging fit to bust and I knew a scamper through the bushes was only a matter of me getting my breath back. I think Ben was in worse shape than me.

"Don't you ever do that again, Pepper, you scared me half to death." Mary Lou sat down next to him. "Well, you know what it's like. If they get a taste for it, there ain't no stopping 'em. But I can rig him up a harness like I use for Voodoo."

My ears pricked up at that. "Don't you dare, Ben. You and me's boulderers. Remember that. Just man, dog and rock."

Mary Lou turned to pat me on the head.

"You hear that? He likes the idea. Come over to my place tonight and I'll get him fitted out." Maybe she just didn't get the Jack Russell accent.

Voodoo jumped off the mat and headed for the trees. I trotted after her, giving Ben a quick head butt on the way past just to remind him that a dog's gotta do what a dog's gotta, but hell, him and me are climbing buddies and that means more than butt-sniffing a bitch any day.

I could hear Mary Lou still burbling away, and Ben too damn stupid to smell the heat. "That was one helluva barnstorming performance."

"Yeah, out-climbed by my dog."

"Well, outflown by your dog, anyway. If you come round to my place, after we've got him all fitted out with a climbing harness, we could all watch that Robert Redford movie, you know, the one about the World War 1 flying ace, I've got it on DVD."

"Which one's that."

Hoots of laughter floated through the trees. "The Great Waldo Pepper, of course".

I nuzzled Voodoo. "Hi, babe, you hear that? That's my name from now on."

"Then I'll call you Waldo." She wagged her tail right in my face. "And afterwards we'll see about the Great."

(Story inspired by Colorado canine climbing aces, Biscuit and Felix.)

HAPPY CLIMBING TELLS NO TALES

Holding her beer up to the light, the woman turned it slowly, letting the sun warm each molecule, coaxing them into subtle flavour. Caught in the prism of the glass, the sunlight struck multi-coloured starbursts through the amber liquid. She tilted her head so that one eye squinted through the clear strip above the foam and saw the blue sky deepening into evening whilst the other saw the garden transformed into a sepia image of a bygone time. She lowered the glass and smiled at her companion.

"The perfect pint."

They chinked their glasses together and each took their first sip, savouring the flavour. She wiped the back of her hand across her mouth.

"Worth waiting for, that"

"A pint to match the climbing. The true essence of the English soul. Cheers."

He tipped back the glass and chugged away at the beer in a steady guzzle. When he put it back onto the table it was already half empty.

"Woa! You're getting way ahead of me."

" Slipping down very easily. Definitely on form tonight."

The landlord came out, collecting glasses and breathing in the warm summer air laden, like the wall of the pub, with the sweet bloom of bush roses. He stood next to the pair, a cloth in one hand and glasses pinched together in the fingers of the other. "Been climbing?"

"Hi Jeff. Yes, great day for it. Good to round it off with one of these." He raised the glass and took a swig.

"It's really on form tonight, Jeff"

The landlord looked over his shoulder, then hunkered down by the table with a conspiratorial air. He spoke in an elaborately loud whisper.

"Could you go and tell that Southern prat over there that this is what good beer is supposed to taste like. He told me it was off and asked me to replace it with lager!"

The man laughed.

"Don't be too hard on him. They're genetically encoded to drink Fosters in the south. I shouldn't worry about it."

Jeff pushed himself up from the table.

"I don't. From a business point of view I'd rather you two were drinking bottled lager as well." He glanced down at the glasses. "I'll start pulling the next round, shall I?"

"Aye – be with you in a minute." She looked at her companion's rapidly diminishing glass. "Maybe less". She screwed up an empty crisp packet into a knot and pushed it towards the man.

"There you are, do your party trick with that, it might slow down your drinking.

He carefully unwrapped it, smoothing the cellophane on the plastic tabletop and folded it in a precise series of tucks and turns to make a neat diamond shape. She held out her hand and he dropped it into her palm.

"Gosh, it's amazing what you can achieve with an expensive education." She pretended to dangle it from her ear. "Oh, I can make an earring!" She licked it and stuck it to her

T-shirt where it hovered for a moment before dropping on the grass. "I can make a brooch!"

"When you find a commercial application for these things let me know so that I can retire a wealthy man".

The woman sat back in the chair and gazed up at the fellside above the pub. It glowed in the late evening sun.

"Fantastic, isn't it? Fancy being able to live here. Fancy just being able to walk up to one of the best crags in Britain and climb classic routes all day and then come down to this. All on our doorstep. God, we're lucky!"

"There are plenty of folk who think we're just plain bonkers."

"Well all the world's bloody strange except thee and me, and recently I've been worried about thee."

The man picked up the crisp wrapper parcel from the grass and tried to stuff it into the hole where the umbrella pole went through the table. The umbrella swayed drunkenly.

"'Ere mind me drink, Sid!"

"Why do these things always lean at an angle?"

"Why do these things always advertise nasty chemically drinks that rot your teeth?"

"Exactly! They should advertise health drinks, like beer."

She noticed a bit of blood on the back of his hand.

"What's that?"

"Stabbed myself with the nut-extractor getting that jammed nut out on Botterill's Slab."

"Proves it's a real climb, that. Shedding blood on it."

"As long as it's only half a teaspoonful."

"Pour some beer on it. It'll be antiseptic."

"I've spat on it. It'll be OK."

Glass in hand, the woman made a sweeping gesture that took in the assembled tourists in the garden.

"This lot" she announced portentously, "probably don't think it counts as real climbing unless you die on it."

She wagged her finger at Sid. "At the very least you could have had the decency to smash both ankles so that you had to crawl down to the pub on hands and knees. I thought you were supposed to be a real climber and here you are with a slight cut where you stabbed yourself with a nut-key. Call yourself a mountaineer!"

Sid licked the back of his hand.

"Yeuch! I'll need some more beer to take away the taste." He waggled his empty glass at her. "Come on, Chrissy, I hate the taste of blood, especially when it's me own."

"Hold yer horses, mate, I've still got a few mouthfuls left. Don't want to rush them." She took a deliberately small sip.

"Bloody Hell, woman. You drink even slower than you climb."

Chrissy extracted the crisp wrapper from the hole and threw it at Sid. The umbrella lurched sideways. "I was savouring it – like me ale! How often do you get such a perfect day on Scafell? Warm, for heaven's sake, and dry. And nobody else on your tail or holding you up? It was too good to hurry. You need days like that to remind you why the hell you climb. When you're on some shivery cold, wet stance, belayed to a twig, it's good to remember days like today."

Sid waved his empty glass at the tourists. "Do you think they would understand that?"

Chrissy shrugged. "How could they? All they hear about is people cutting ropes and dying en masse on Everest. They don't hear the good stories. Mates going out and just having a good time. And the feel of the rock. And working out the moves. And the views."

"And the beer?" hinted Sid.

"Oh, alright! Pass us your glass."

He slid it across the table, narrowly avoiding the umbrella pole. Chrissy picked it up and half rose from her seat.

"It's a shame no-one writes about the ninety-nine times out of a hundred that climbing is fun and no-one gets hurt."

"Well, there's no story in it, is there?"

"How d'you mean?"

"There's no dramatic tension if everything goes right. It would be like trying to write a novel about a happy marriage. Just wouldn't work. Anyway, climbers are their own worst enemies. We're a right bunch of drama queens. We'd make an epic out of a *trip to the bar* to get a story out of it." He put a heavy emphasis on the salient words.

"OK, I'm going."

She stood up and picked up both glasses.

"Happy climbing tells no tales, death and terror get the sales."

"That's good. Where did you get that from?"

"Out of me head. Just now. It's me own compose-ion, you know."

"Well, buy me another beer and we'll drink to epics and long may they be figments of our over-heated imaginations."

"Alright, I'm making the summit push now. Same again?"

"How long have we been climbing together, Chrissy?"

"O.K., silly bloody question. If I'm not back in 15 minutes, call the rescue, I've probably tripped over a lager-drinker."

"You get a good photo of the corpse and I'll write the article" said Sid.

Printed in the United Kingdom
by Lightning Source UK Ltd.
124177UK00001B/454-591/A